10 9 8 7 6 5 4 3 2 1

First published in 2003 by BBC Books, an imprint of Ebury Publishing
A Random House Group Company. This revised edition published 2014.

Recipes © BBC Worldwide 2003
Photographs © BBC Worldwide 2003
Book design © Woodlands Books Ltd 2014
All the recipes contained in this book first appeared in BBC Good Food magazine

The Random House Group Ltd Reg. No. 954009

Addresses for companies within the Random House Group Ltd can be found at www.randomhouse.co.uk

A CIP catalogue record for this book is available from the British Library.

The Random House Group Limited supports the Forest Stewardship Council® (FSC®), the leading international forest-certification organisation. Our books carrying the FSC label are printed on FSC®-certified paper. FSC is the only forest-certification scheme supported by the leading environmental organisations, including Greenpeace. Our paper procurement policy can be found at www.randomhouse.co.uk/environment

To buy books by your favourite authors and register for offers visit www.randomhouse.co.uk

Edited by Barney Desmazery
Commissioning Editor: Lizzy Gray
Project Editor: Lizzy Gaisford
Designers: Interstate Creative Partners Ltd
Design Manager: Kathryn Gammon
Production: Alex Goddard
Picture Researcher: Gabby Harrington

MIX
Paper from
responsible sources
FSC® C004592
www.fsc.org

Printed and bound by Firmengruppe APPL, aprinta druck, Wemding, Germany
Colour origination by Dot Gradations Ltd, UK

ISBN 9781849908689

PICTURE CREDITS

BBC Good Food magazine and BBC Books would like to thank the following people for providing photos. While every effort has been made to trace and acknowledge all photographers, we should like to apologise should there be any errors or omissions.

Chris Alack p159, p181, p203; Marie-Louise Avery p103; Iain Bagwell p89; Clive Bozzard-Hill p31, p63, p199; Peter Cassidy p49, p97, p205, p211; Ken Field p51, p109, p115 ; Will Heap p59, p87, p131, p141, p155; Dave King p189; Richard Kolker p23, p41, p119; Adrian Lawrence p101; Gareth Morgans p15, p127; David Munns p25, p21, p47, p65, p69, p157, p197, p201, p207; Myles New p61, p117, p125, p147; Thomas Odulate p153, p193; Stuart Ovenden p17, p139, p187; Lis Parsons p121; William Reavell p11, p107, p133, p137, p151, p169, p183, p191, p195; Howard Shooter p29, Simon Smith p99; Roger Stowell p27, p35, p39, p111, p145; Sam Stowell p13, p19, p33, p37, p45, p71, p75, p81, p83, p93, p113, p123, p135, p143, p161, p171, p175, p209; Rob Streeter p53; Mark Thompson p129; Trevor Vaughan p57, p67, p77, p105, p185; Philip Webb p43, p149; Simon Wheeler p73, p85; Frank Wieder p63, p79, p91, p95, p179; BBC Worldwide p55, p173, p177

All the recipes in this book were created by the editorial team at Good Food and by regular contributors to BBC Magazines.

BBC

goodfood
VEGGIE DISHES

BBC goodfood
VEGGIE DISHES

Editor **Orlando Murrin**

BOOKS

Contents

Introduction

Whether you're a lifelong devotee or someone who wants a change for one night, there's much more to veggie cooking than a cheese omelette or a mushroom risotto. Vegetarian food should be a celebration of global flavours and seasonal ingredients and in this revised and updated edition we have the perfect collection of delicious recipes that prove that fact. It's got all those simple-but-delectable vegetarian recipes you always wish you had up your sleeve. We think you'll find it invaluable whatever the occasion, with ideas on light snacks, mains and puds, plus the trickiest dishes of all – dairy-free.

All the recipes have been tested in the Good Food kitchen, guaranteeing you success every time. They're also well balanced and come with a nutritional breakdown so you can keep track of the calorie, fat and salt content.

As always, our recipes make the most of vegetables in season plus good use of storecupboard and frozen vegetables, which count towards your five-a-day recommended portions of fruit and vegetables. So, not only will you wow family and friends with fabulous food, like *Melanzane parmigiana* pictured opposite (see page 156 for the recipe), they'll be getting healthy, balanced meals into the bargain.

Orlando Murrin

Orlando Murrin
BBC *Good Food* Magazine

Notes &
Conversion Tables

. . . .

- Eggs are large in the UK and Australia and extra large in America unless stated.
- Wash fresh produce before preparation.
- Recipes contain nutritional analyses for 'sugar', which means the total sugar content including all natural sugars in the ingredients, unless otherwise stated.

OVEN TEMPERATURES

GAS	°C	°C FAN	°F	OVEN TEMP.
¼	110	90	225	Very cool
½	120	100	250	Very cool
1	140	120	275	Cool or slow
2	150	130	300	Cool or slow
3	160	140	325	Warm
4	180	160	350	Moderate
5	190	170	375	Moderately hot
6	200	180	400	Fairly hot
7	220	200	425	Hot
8	230	210	450	Very hot
9	240	220	475	Very hot

APPROXIMATE WEIGHT CONVERSIONS

- All the recipes in this book list both imperial and metric measurements. Conversions are approximate and have been rounded up or down. Follow one set of measurements only; do not mix the two.
- Cup measurements, which are used in Australia and America, have not been listed here as they vary from ingredient to ingredient. Kitchen scales should be used to measure dry/solid ingredients.

Good Food is concerned about sustainable sourcing and animal welfare. Where possible, humanely reared meats, sustainably caught fish (see fishonline.org for further information from the Marine Conservation Society) and free-range chickens and eggs are used when recipes are originally tested.

SPOON MEASURES

Spoon measurements are level unless otherwise specified.

- 1 teaspoon (tsp) = 5ml
- 1 tablespoon (tbsp) = 15ml
- 1 Australian tablespoon = 20ml (cooks in Australia should measure 3 teaspoons where 1 tablespoon is specified in a recipe)

APPROXIMATE LIQUID CONVERSIONS

METRIC	IMPERIAL	AUS	US
50ml	2fl oz	¼ cup	¼ cup
125ml	4fl oz	½ cup	½ cup
175ml	6fl oz	¾ cup	¾ cup
225ml	8fl oz	1 cup	1 cup
300ml	10fl oz/½ pint	½ pint	1¼ cups
450ml	16fl oz	2 cups	2 cups/1 pint
600ml	20fl oz/1 pint	1 pint	2½ cups
1 litre	35fl oz/1¾ pints	1¾ pints	1 quart

Spinach, sage & potato soup

A velvety smooth soup with a dramatic colour but gentle flavour.

 40 minutes 4

- 50g/2oz butter
- 2 red onions, chopped
- 3 garlic cloves, crushed
- 15g sage leaves, shredded, plus extra to garnish
- 2 large potatoes (about 500g/1lb 2oz total), diced
- 1.4 litres/2½ pints vegetable stock
- 250g/9oz baby leaf spinach
- 4 tbsp crème fraîche, to garnish (optional)

1 Melt the butter in a large pan and fry the onions for 5–6 minutes over a low heat until softened slightly. Add the garlic, sage and potatoes, cover and cook over a very low heat for 10 minutes.

2 Stir in the stock, bring to the boil and cook for 5 minutes. Add the spinach and cook for 2 minutes. Transfer the mixture to a food processor or blender and whizz until smooth (you may need to do this in batches).

3 Return the soup to the pan and heat gently until warmed. Season to taste and serve with a spoonful of crème fraîche, if using, garnished with the extra sage.

PER SERVING 265 kcals, protein 7g, carbs 28g, fat 14g, sat fat 9g, fibre 4g, sugar none, salt 1.67g

Cauliflower & apple soup

Take two classic British ingredients and whip up a big batch of this comforting soup to feed a crowd or to eat throughout the week.

 30 minutes 8

- 50g/2oz butter
- 4 onions, thinly sliced
- 1.5kg/3lb 5oz cauliflower (about 2 large cauliflowers), broken into very small florets
- 8 eating apples, 6 cored, peeled and chopped, 2 unpeeled and cut into matchsticks (squeeze over lemon juice to prevent browning)
- 2 vegetable stock cubes, crumbled
- 1.5 litres/2¾ pints milk
- 8 tbsp single cream
- olive oil, for drizzling
- few fresh thyme sprigs, leaves picked, to garnish

1 Melt the butter in a pan, add the onions and fry gently until softened. Add the cauliflower and chopped apple, and fry for 5 minutes. Add the stock cubes and milk, and bring to the boil, then reduce to a simmer and cook for 5 minutes, or until the cauliflower and apples are tender.

2 Use a hand blender or liquidiser to purée the soup until smooth and season (the soup can now be chilled for up to 48 hours or frozen for up to 3 months, just defrost and reheat to serve). Divide into bowls and swirl 1 tablespoon of the cream in each along with a drizzle of oil. Top with the apple matchsticks and thyme.

PER SERVING 284 kcals, protein 15g, carbs 27g, fat 13g, sat fat 8g, fibre 7g, sugar 24g, salt 1.1g

Springtime minestrone

· · · · · · · · · · · · · · · · · · · ·

This quick soup is made with only five ingredients and makes clever use of leftover cooked pasta.

 15 minutes 4

- 200g/8oz mixed green vegetables (we used asparagus, broad beans, spring onions and green beans)
- 700ml/1¼ pint hot vegetable stock
- 140g/5oz cooked pasta (spaghetti works well, chopped into small pieces)
- 215g can butter beans, drained and rinsed
- 3 tbsp basil pesto
- crusty bread, to serve

1 Prepare the vegetables, cutting larger veg into bite-sized pieces. Put in a medium-sized pan, then pour over the stock. Bring to the boil, then reduce the heat and simmer until the vegetables are cooked through, about 3 minutes.

2 Stir in the cooked pasta, beans and 1 tablespoon of the pesto. Warm through, then ladle into bowls and top each with an extra drizzle of pesto. Serve with some crusty bread.

· ·
PER SERVING 125 kcals, protein 8g, carbs 16g, fat 4g, sat fat 1g, fibre 4g, sugar 3g, salt 0.7g

Curried squash, lentil & coconut soup

Make more than you need of this dairy-free, vegan-friendly soup, and you'll have a filling lunch to take to work the next day.

 35 minutes    6

- 1 tbsp olive oil
- 1 butternut squash, peeled, deseeded and diced
- 200g/8oz carrots, diced
- 1 tbsp mild curry powder containing turmeric
- 100g/4oz red split lentils
- 700ml/1¼ pint vegetable stock
- 400ml can reduced-fat coconut milk
- roughly chopped coriander, to garnish
- naan bread, to serve

1 Heat the oil in a large pan, add the squash and carrots, sizzle for 1 minute, then stir in the curry powder and cook for 1 minute more. Tip in the lentils, vegetable stock and coconut milk, and give everything a good stir. Bring to the boil, then turn the heat down and simmer for 15–20 minutes until everything is tender.

2 Using a hand blender or food processor, blitz until as smooth as you like. Season and reheat if you need to. Serve scattered with roughly chopped coriander and some naan bread alongside.

PER SERVING 178 kcals, protein 6g, carbs 22g, fat 7g, sat fat 5g, fibre 4g, sugar 9g, salt 0.4g

Tomato & rice soup

This budget-friendly, filling soup is cleverly made using storecupboard staples, so it's a great standby recipe when your fridge is bare.

 45 minutes 4

- 2 tsp olive oil
- 1 onion, finely chopped
- 1 carrot, finely chopped
- 1 celery stick, finely chopped
- 1 tbsp golden caster sugar
- 2 tbsp vinegar (white, red or balsamic)
- 1 tbsp tomato purée
- 400g can chopped tomatoes or passata
- 1 litre/1¾ pints vegetable stock made with 2 cubes
- 140g/5oz rice (white long grain or basmati, wild, brown or a mixture)
- ¼ small pack parsley, leaves only, chopped, to garnish
- a few dollops of basil pesto, to swirl (optional)

1 Heat the oil in a large pan and add the onion, carrot and celery, then cook gently until softened. Add the sugar and vinegar, cook for 1 minute, then stir through the tomato purée. Add the chopped tomatoes or passata and the vegetable stock. If you are using brown rice, add it now. Cover and simmer for 10 minutes. Then add any wild rice and simmer for 10 minutes more. Finally, add the white rice, if using, and simmer for another 10 minutes until the rice is tender.

2 Just before serving, sprinkle over some chopped parsley and season to taste. Divide into bowls and add a swirl of pesto to each, if you like.

PER SERVING 213 kcals, protein 6g, carbs 39g, fat 3g, sat fat 1g, fibre 4g, sugar 13g, salt 1.6g

Celeriac salad with Parmesan, walnuts & parsley

Make sure you toss raw celeriac with lemon juice as soon as it's prepared – not only does this keep it white, but it softens it slightly as well.

 15 minutes 4

- juice 1 lemon
- ½ celeriac, peeled, and cut into sixths
- 2 celery sticks from the inner bunch, leaves left on
- small pack flat-leaf parsley, leaves picked
- handful walnut halves, toasted
- 1 tbsp olive oil, plus extra to drizzle
- 50g/2oz Parmesan (or vegetarian alternative), shaved with a vegetable peeler

FOR THE DRESSING
- 1 tbsp wholegrain mustard
- 3 tbsp olive oil
- 1 tbsp sherry vinegar

1 First make the dressing. Whisk all the ingredients together with 1 tablespoon water and some seasoning, and set aside.
2 Tip the lemon juice into a bowl. Use a swivel-blade peeler to shave thin ribbons of celeriac into the lemon juice and toss to coat.
3 Thinly slice the celery sticks on an angle, but keep the leaves on. Toss all the remaining ingredients, except the Parmesan, with the celeriac and season with sea salt and a little black pepper.
4 Pile the salad on to four plates and top with the Parmesan shavings. Drizzle with the dressing and extra olive oil before serving.

PER SERVING 269 kcals, protein 8g, carbs 3g, fat 25g, sat fat 5g, fibre 6g, sugar 2g, salt 0.8g

Hot mushroom & kumquat salad

Tangy kumquats contrast with the earthy flavours of the mushrooms and sweet red onion.

 30 minutes   2   Easily doubled

- 5 tbsp olive oil
- 250g/9oz mixed mushrooms, (such as field, shiitake, chestnut), sliced
- 1 red onion, sliced
- 50g/2oz kumquats, sliced
- pinch dried chilli flakes
- 50g/2oz sliced white bread, crusts removed and cubed
- 85g/3oz rocket leaves
- 1 tbsp white wine vinegar

1 Melt 1 tablespoon of the oil in a frying pan and fry the mushrooms for 2–3 minutes. Add the onion and kumquats, and fry for a further 2–3 minutes. Set aside and keep warm.

2 Mix together the chilli flakes, bread cubes and 1 tablespoon of the oil in a small bowl. Season well. Heat 1 tablespoon of the oil in the frying pan and fry the bread mixture until crisp and golden. Divide the rocket between serving plates and top with the mushroom-and-kumquat mix and the chilli croutons.

3 Whisk together the last of the oil with the vinegar, season, and drizzle over the salad. Serve immediately.

PER SERVING 488 kcals, protein 6g, carbs 19g, fat 39g, sat fat 6g, fibre 4g, sugar none, salt 0.46g

Two-cheese salad with croutons

Use less salty Lancashire cheese in place of feta, if you prefer.

 30 minutes 4

- 2 thick slices white bread, crusts removed
- 1 tsp paprika
- 2 tbsp olive oil
- 1 garlic clove, crushed
- 1 large cos or romaine lettuce
- 2 ripe avocados
- 2 tbsp lemon juice
- 1 large courgette, cut into sticks
- 140g/5oz feta, crumbled into chunks
- 25g/1oz finely grated Parmesan
- 6 tbsp olive oil dressing (ready-made)

1 Heat oven to 220C/200C fan/gas 7. Cut the bread into 2cm/¾in cubes. Toss with the paprika, olive oil and garlic, then spread out on a baking sheet. Bake for 7–8 minutes, until crisp.

2 Meanwhile, tear the lettuce into large pieces. Peel and slice the avocados and toss with lemon juice and some freshly ground black pepper.

3 Mix the lettuce, courgette, feta and croutons in a large salad bowl, add the avocado, and sprinkle with Parmesan. Drizzle olive oil dressing over the salad to serve.

PER SERVING 453 kcals, protein 12g, carbs 12g, fat 40g, sat fat 10g, fibre 4g, sugar none, salt 1.92g

English garden salad

A fresh-tasting salad made from summer vegetables, crumbly cheese and mint.

 30 minutes 4

- 500g/1lb 2oz new potatoes, sliced thickly
- 350g/12oz runner beans, sliced
- bunch spring onions, chopped
- 240g tub SunBlush or sun-dried tomatoes, drained
- 200g/8oz Cheshire or Lancashire cheese
- good handful mint leaves, roughly chopped
- 4–5 tbsp shop-bought honey and mustard dressing

1 Cook the potatoes in salted boiling water for 7 minutes. Add the beans to the pan and cook for a further 7–9 minutes, until the potatoes and beans are just tender.
2 Drain the vegetables and rinse under cold running water to stop them cooking. Shake the colander to get rid of as much water as possible, then tip into a large bowl. Add the onions and tomatoes, crumble in the cheese and mix well.
3 Add most of the mint and dressing, and toss everything lightly together. Tip into a serving dish, drizzle with a little more dressing and scatter over the rest of the mint.

PER SERVING 427 kcals, protein 18g, carbs 29g, fat 27g, sat fat 11g, fibre 6g, sugar none, salt 2.39g

Feta & griddled peach salad

Check the cheese counter in the supermarket for jars of marinated feta in oil. Use the oil for the dressing.

 10 minutes 4

- juice 1 lime
- 4 fresh ripe peaches, each cut into wedges
- 200g bag mixed salad leaves
- 300g jar marinated feta in oil
- 1 red onion, sliced
- 2 tbsp chopped mint leaves

1 Heat a lightly greased griddle pan until very hot. Squeeze the lime juice over the peaches and put them on the griddle pan. Cook the peaches for 2–3 minutes, turning, until nicely charred.

2 In a large salad bowl, mix together the salad leaves, feta, 2 tablespoons of the oil from the feta, the red onion and chopped mint. Season well.

3 Divide among plates and top with the charred peaches. Sprinkle over black pepper and serve.

PER SERVING 272 kcals, protein 11g, carbs 11g, fat 21g, sat fat 9g, fibre 2g, sugar none, salt 2.32g

Goat's cheese salad

Choose a small, soft goat's cheese. The rind is edible but discard the ends to make four matching slices.

 10 minutes   1    Easily multiplied

- 100g/4oz soft goat's cheese
- 1 oval bread roll, cut into 4 slices and ends discarded
- 4 tsp olive oil
- 1 tsp lemon juice or white wine vinegar
- ½ tsp wholegrain or Dijon mustard
- 1 garlic clove, chopped
- handful mixed salad leaves

1 Heat grill to high. Cut the cheese into four slices. Toast the bread slices on both sides, then top with the cheese.
2 Sprinkle the cheese toasts with some black pepper and a little of the olive oil, and grill for 2–3 minutes.
3 Meanwhile, mix together the remaining olive oil, the lemon juice or vinegar, mustard and garlic in a small bowl. Season, then toss with the salad leaves. Pile on to a plate and top with the cheese toasts.

PER SERVING 509 kcals, protein 19g, carbs 16g, fat 42g, sat fat 15g, fibre 1g, sugar none, salt 1.84g

Roasted beetroot & egg salad

This substantial salad would make a great weekend lunch in the garden, or you can bulk it out with a few more leaves and serve it as a starter for four.

 30-35 minutes 2

- 200g/8oz vacuum-packed cooked beetroot, cut into wedges
- 2 tbsp olive oil
- 3 tsp sherry vinegar
- 1 tbsp clear honey
- 2 eggs
- 2 tbsp crème fraîche
- 1 tsp Dijon mustard
- a few dill stalks, most finely chopped, a few small fronds picked for garnish
- 70g bag lamb's lettuce
- 1 tbsp roasted chopped hazelnuts

1 Heat oven to 200C/180C fan/gas 6. Pop the beetroot in a roasting tin, add half the oil, 2 teaspoons of the vinegar, the honey and some seasoning. Roast for 20–25 minutes, tossing twice until sticky. Leave to cool for a few minutes.

2 Meanwhile, put the eggs in boiling water. Turn down the heat and simmer for 10 minutes, then run under cold water to cool. Peel and halve.

3 Mix the remaining oil, crème fraîche, mustard, the final teaspoon of vinegar and the chopped dill together in a large bowl. Toss the lamb's lettuce in the dressing and arrange on plates with the roasted beetroot and egg. Scatter with a few dill fronds and tumble over the nuts.

PER SERVING 363 kcals, protein 11g, carbs 18g, fat 28g, sat fat 8g, fibre 4g, sugar 17g, salt 0.7g

Feta & flageolet salad

Use authentic Greek feta for the best flavour. It keeps for about 6 months unopened in the fridge, so it's a great supper standby.

 10–20 minutes   4

- 100g/4oz baby leaf spinach
- 300g/10oz large salad tomatoes, cut into wedges
- 400g can flageolet or cannellini beans, drained and rinsed
- 1 small red onion, finely chopped
- 200g pack feta
- crusty bread, to serve

FOR THE DRESSING

- 1 garlic clove, finely chopped
- 1 tbsp lemon juice
- 1 tsp clear honey
- 3 tbsp olive oil

1 Cover a large platter or shallow dish with the spinach leaves. Scatter the tomato wedges over the spinach, followed by the beans and red onion.
2 Drain off the liquid from the pack of feta and crumble the cheese over the vegetables.
3 Tip the dressing ingredients into a small bowl, season and whisk with a fork until slightly thickened. Drizzle over the salad, and serve with crusty bread.

PER SERVING 515 kcals, protein 31g, carbs 56g, fat 20g, sat fat 8g, fibre 19g, sugar 1g, salt 2.05g

Quinoa, squash & broccoli salad

This healthy salad will keep in the fridge for 2 days, making it ideal to take to work for lunch or just to have ready to graze on when you're peckish.

 20 minutes 2

- 2 tsp rapeseed oil
- 1 red onion, halved and sliced
- 2 garlic cloves, sliced
- 175g/6oz frozen butternut squash chunks
- 140g/5oz broccoli, stalks sliced, top cut into small florets
- 1 tbsp thyme leaves
- 250g pack ready-to-eat red & white quinoa
- 2 tbsp chopped flat-leaf parsley
- 25g/1oz dried cranberries
- handful pumpkin seeds (optional)
- 1 tbsp balsamic vinegar
- 50g/2oz feta, crumbled

1 Heat the oil in a wok with a lid, add the onion and garlic, and fry for 5 minutes until softened, then lift from the wok with a slotted spoon. Add the squash, cook, stirring, until it starts to colour, then add the broccoli. Sprinkle in 3 tablespoons water and the thyme, cover the wok and steam for about 5 minutes until the veg is tender.

2 Meanwhile, tip the quinoa into a bowl and fluff it up. Add the parsley, cranberries, seeds (if using), cooked onion and garlic, and balsamic vinegar, and mix well. Toss through the vegetables with the feta and serve, or chill for later.

PER SERVING 475 kcals, protein 17g, carbs 64g, fat 17g, sat fat 5g, fibre 10g, sugar 21g, salt 1.8g

Greek pasta salad

The traditional combination of tomatoes, olives and feta cheese is made more substantial by the addition of pasta.

 30 minutes 4

- 300g/10oz fusilli (spirals) or farfalle (butterflies) or penne (quill tubes)
- 225g bag baby leaf spinach
- 250g punnet cherry tomatoes, halved
- 100g/4oz Kalamata olives
- 200g/8oz feta, broken into rough chunks
- 3 tbsp olive oil
- crusty bread, to serve

1 Tip the pasta into a large pan of salted boiling water and boil for 10 minutes. Throw in the spinach, stir well and boil for another 2 minutes. Drain into a colander or sieve and leave to drip dry.

2 Tip the tomatoes, olives and feta into a large bowl, grind lots of black pepper over and then drizzle with the olive oil.

3 Toss in the drained pasta and spinach, and serve with crusty bread.

PER SERVING 418 kcals, protein 18g, carbs 37g, fat 23g, sat fat 8g, fibre 5g, sugar 1g, salt 3.48g

Beetroot & tzatziki sandwich

Tzatziki is Greek yogurt and cucumber salad, usually eaten as a dip for pitta bread.

 10 minutes   1   Easily multiplied

- knob softened butter
- 2 thick slices mixed-seed bread
- 3 tbsp low fat Greek yogurt
- 4cm/1½in piece cucumber, grated and drained
- 2 tbsp chopped mint leaves, plus extra whole leaves to garnish
- handful mixed salad leaves
- 1 small cooked beetroot, sliced

1 Spread the softened butter over one side of each slice of bread.

2 To make the tzatziki, mix together the Greek yogurt, grated cucumber and chopped mint in a small bowl. Season well.

3 Put a handful of mixed salad leaves on each slice of bread. Arrange the beetroot slices on top of the salad leaves and spoon over the cucumber tzatziki. Sprinkle with the extra fresh mint leaves.

PER SERVING 433 kcals, protein 13g, carbs 60g, fat 18g, sat fat 11g, fibre 2g, sugar none, salt 1.63g

Blue cheese, butternut & barley salad with maple walnuts

· ·

Not all cheese is suitable for vegetarians, so check the packaging first.

 55 minutes 6

- 1 butternut squash, peeled and cut into chunks, seeds reserved
- 2 red onions, cut into quarters
- 3 garlic cloves, peeled and bashed
- 3½ tbsp extra virgin olive oil
- handful thyme sprigs, leaves stripped, plus extra to garnish
- 300g/10oz pearl barley
- 50g/2oz walnuts, roughly chopped
- 1½ tbsp maple syrup
- 1 tsp brown sugar
- ½ tsp chilli flakes
- 2 tsp balsamic vinegar
- 1 tsp Dijon mustard
- 100g/4oz baby leaf spinach, shredded
- 140g/5oz blue cheese, thinly sliced

1 Heat oven to 200C/180C fan/gas 6. Toss the squash, onions and garlic with 2 tablespoons of the oil and season. Roast for 35–45 minutes – turning halfway through cooking and adding the thyme leaves. Remove from the oven and allow to cool, discarding the garlic.

2 Cook the barley, according to the pack instructions, until just cooked. Drain and cool.

3 Meanwhile, rinse the squash seeds, removing any flesh, and dry. Toast the walnuts and squash seeds in a frying pan until golden. Add ½ tablespoon of the oil, the maple syrup, sugar, chilli flakes and some salt. Bubble for a few minutes, until caramelised. Tip on to a baking sheet, allow to cool, then bash into pieces. Make a dressing by mixing the vinegar, mustard and remaining oil. Season.

4 Toss the squash mix through the barley, followed by the spinach and dressing. Scatter over the cheese, caramelised nuts and seeds and garnish with thyme sprigs to serve.

· ·

PER SERVING 479 kcals, protein 14g, carbs 57g, fat 22g, sat fat 7g, fibre 3g, sugar 12g, salt 0.7g

Halloumi & tomato pitta

· · · · · · · · · · · · · · · · · · · ·

Grill the halloumi cheese until just golden and eat it immediately as it becomes chewy when it cools.

 10 minutes   1   Easily multiplied

- 2 cos lettuce leaves, shredded
- 1 plum tomato, sliced
- 1 thin slice sweet onion, separated into rings
- 1 mint sprig, chopped
- 1 tsp olive oil
- 3 thick slices halloumi
- 1 pitta bread

1 Heat grill to high. Put the lettuce, tomato slices, onion rings and mint in a bowl, toss together with the olive oil and season.

2 Put the halloumi slices on a baking sheet and grill for about 2 minutes until turning golden then turn over and grill for a further minute.

3 Grill the pitta pocket for a few seconds on each side until it puffs open. Tuck the cheese and salad inside the pitta. Eat straight away.

· ·

PER SERVING 375 kcals, protein 16g, carbs 46g, fat 15g, sat fat 7g, fibre 3g, sugar none, salt 1.45g

Lighter nachos

Who doesn't love a big dish of nachos? Well, here's a healthier version so you can now enjoy them without any guilt.

 50 minutes 4  Easily doubled

- 5 soft corn tortillas
- 1½ tsp rapeseed oil
- 1 jalapeño chilli, deseeded, cut into thin strips
- 100g/4oz mozzarella, grated
- 2 tbsp half-fat crème fraîche
- ½ small pack coriander leaves, chopped
- tub guacamole, to serve

FOR THE BEANS
- 400g can red kidney beans, drained and rinsed
- 1 garlic clove, crushed
- ¼ tsp mild or medium chilli powder
- ¼ tsp ground cumin

FOR THE SALSA
- 4 tomatoes, seeds removed, finely chopped
- ¼ small red onion, finely chopped
- 1 garlic clove, finely chopped
- 1 tbsp lime juice
- 1 tsp rapeseed oil

1 Heat oven to 190C/170C fan/gas 5. For each tortilla, brush both sides with some oil and cut into 12 wedges. Repeat. Bake the wedges on two large baking sheets for 10 minutes until golden and crisp. Remove and set aside. Turn oven to 200C/180C fan/gas 6.

2 For the beans, tip them into a bowl, stir in the garlic, chilli and cumin powders, and roughly mash with a fork. Mix in about 2 tablespoons water or enough to make a rough mash. Season and set aside.

3 For the salsa, combine the tomatoes, onion, garlic, lime juice and oil. Season.

4 Some 10 minutes before you're ready to serve, scatter the tortilla chips over a large baking sheet or ovenproof platter. Spoon the beans in little mounds over the chips, then spoon over the salsa. Scatter over the jalapeño chilli and mozzarella. Bake for 4–5 minutes, being careful not to overbrown the tortilla chips. Remove, spoon over the crème fraîche and scatter with coriander. Serve immediately with the guacamole on the side.

PER SERVING 462 kcals, protein 15g, carbs 41g, fat 27g, sat fat 9g, fibre 9g, sugar 7g, salt 1.6g

Broccoli & poached egg toasts

If you can't find purple-sprouting broccoli, use green broccoli cut into thin florets.

 25 minutes 4

- 200g/8oz purple-sprouting broccoli
- 1 ciabatta loaf
- 1 garlic clove, halved
- 2 tbsp olive oil
- 1 tbsp Dijon mustard
- 6 shallots, halved lengthways
- 4 eggs

1 Slice the broccoli and blanch in boiling water for 1 minute. Drain and refresh in cold water. Dry on kitchen paper. Heat a griddle or frying pan.

2 Cut the ciabatta in half horizontally, then cut each slice in half. Rub with the garlic and brush with half the oil. Cook the ciabatta on the griddle or in the pan for 1–2 minutes on each side until golden. Spread with the mustard and keep warm. Toss the shallots in the remaining olive oil and cook cut-side down on the griddle or in the pan for 2 minutes on each side. Keep warm.

3 Pile the broccoli on to the griddle or pan and cook for 3–4 minutes, turning frequently. Meanwhile, poach the eggs in gently simmering water until set to your liking. Pile the shallots and broccoli on the ciabatta. Top with the eggs and season.

PER SERVING 380 kcals, protein 17g, carbs 47g, fat 15g, sat fat 3g, fibre 4g, sugar none, salt 1.49g

Olive & ricotta pâté

You should find all these ingredients at the delicatessen counter. Buy some good bread to go with it.

 40 minutes  6

- oil, for greasing
- 450g/1lb ricotta
- 50g/2oz vegetarian Parmesan, finely grated
- 2 medium egg whites, lightly beaten
- 190g jar lemon-and-mint marinated green olives
- 185g can pitted black olives, drained
- 4 sun-dried tomatoes, roughly chopped
- 2 rosemary sprigs, leaves only
- bread and roasted tomatoes, to serve

1 Heat oven to 200C/180C fan/gas 6. Oil and base line a 20cm sandwich tin. In a large bowl, beat together the ricotta, Parmesan, egg whites and some seasoning.
2 Spoon into the prepared tin and level the surface with the back of a wet spoon. Press the olives, sun-dried tomatoes and rosemary into the surface, and bake for 25–30 minutes until firm.
3 Turn out and remove the paper. Serve in wedges with bread and roasted tomatoes.

PER SERVING 227 kcals, protein 12g, carbs 3g, fat 19g, sat fat 8g, fibre 2g, sugar none, salt 4.07g

Mushroom fajitas with avocado houmous

· ·

These wraps are so packed with vegetables that just one serving gives you four of your 5-a-day fruit-and-veg quota.

 35 minutes  2

- 1 large avocado, stoned, peeled and chopped
- 400g can chickpeas, drained and rinsed
- 1 garlic clove, crushed
- zest and juice 1 lemon
- 2 tomatoes, deseeded and diced
- 1 red onion, cut into thick rounds
- 2 large flat mushrooms, thickly sliced
- 2 tbsp olive oil
- 2 tsp fajita spice mix
- 4 tortillas
- shredded Little Gem lettuce and Tabasco sauce, to serve (optional)

1 Put the avocado, chickpeas, garlic, lemon zest and juice in a food processor, and whizz together until it forms a chunky consistency. Spoon the avocado houmous into a bowl, season and stir in the tomatoes.

2 Drizzle the onion and mushrooms with the oil and sprinkle over the fajita seasoning. Heat a griddle pan over a high heat and cook the onion for 2 minutes on each side, then remove from the pan and keep warm. Cook the mushrooms for 2 minutes on each side or until softened and turning golden in places.

3 Spread some of the avocado houmous down the middle of each tortilla and top with the mushrooms and onions. Add shredded lettuce and a dash of Tabasco, if you like, and wrap up.

· ·

PER FAJITA 824 kcals, protein 23g, carbs 104g, fat 36g, sat fat 6g, fibre 14g, sugar 11g, salt 2.3g

Stir-fried salad with almonds

Sounds strange, but take the pan off the heat before you add the salad ingredients and you'll love the fresh-tasting result.

 15 minutes   4

- 3 tbsp olive oil
- 85g/3oz whole blanched almonds
- 1 bunch spring onions, sliced
- 1 small cucumber, seeded and sliced
- 3 celery sticks, cut into batons
- 200g/8oz small tomatoes, quartered
- 2 Little Gem lettuces, torn in pieces
- 25g/1oz watercress leaves
- 25g/1oz coriander leaves
- juice ½ lemon
- ½ tsp sugar
- crusty bread or boiled rice, to serve

1 Heat 2 tablespoons of the oil in a frying pan or wok and fry the almonds for 2–3 minutes until golden. Drain on kitchen paper then chop roughly. Set aside.

2 Add the remaining oil to the pan and, when hot, add the spring onions, cucumber, celery and tomatoes, and stir-fry for 2 minutes. Remove from the heat, add the remaining ingredients and toss together until combined. Season.

3 Spoon the warm salad on to serving plates and scatter the almonds over. Spoon the pan juices over and serve with crusty bread or boiled rice, if liked.

PER SERVING 247 kcals, protein 6g, carbs 6g, fat 22g, sat fat 2g, fibre 3g, sugar 1g, salt 0.09g

Vegetable-blini stacks

Blinis make brilliant bases for canapés and starters. Try them with herby cream cheese, tomatoes and rocket too.

 20 minutes 4

- 200g/8oz asparagus spears, trimmed
- 100g/4oz sugar snap peas
- 140g/5oz broccoli florets
- 250ml tub crème fraîche
- 1½ tbsp fresh vegetarian pesto
- handful basil leaves, roughly torn
- 8 large ready-made blinis (about 10cm/4in diameter)
- 140g/5oz semi-dried tomatoes, drained

1 Heat oven to 180C/160C fan/gas 4. Bring a large pan of salted water to the boil. Add the asparagus, sugar snap peas and broccoli, and cook for 2 minutes until just tender. Drain and set aside. Combine the crème fraîche, pesto and half the basil. Season to taste.
2 Put 4 of the blinis in a large ovenproof dish. Top with the vegetables and tomatoes, and spoon over the crème-fraîche mixture.
3 Halve the remaining blinis and put on top of the vegetables. Bake for 8 minutes until heated through.

PER SERVING 372 kcals, protein 10g, carbs 20g, fat 28g, sat fat 13g, fibre 4g, sugar none, salt 0.43g

Feta & semi-dried tomato omelette

· · · · · · · · · · · · · · · · · · · ·

If you only have sun-dried tomatoes, they'll need soaking in warm water to soften them before chopping.

 10 minutes   1

- 1 tsp olive oil
- 2 eggs, lightly beaten
- 4 semi-dried tomatoes, roughly chopped
- 25g/1oz feta, crumbled
- mixed leaf salad, to serve

1 Heat the oil in a small frying pan, add the eggs and cook, swirling the eggs with a fork as they set. When the eggs are still slightly runny in the middle, scatter over the tomatoes and feta, then fold the omelette in half. Cook for 1 minute more before sliding on to a plate. Serve alongside a mixed leaf salad.

· ·
PER SERVING 266 kcals, protein 18g, carbs 5g, fat 20g, sat fat 7g, fibre 1g, sugar 4g, salt 1.8g

Spicy vegetable chapatti wraps

Curry can be deceivingly high in fat – this version is packed with flavour and has only 5g fat per serving.

 25 minutes   4

- 300g/10oz sweet potatoes, peeled and roughly cubed
- 400g can peeled plum tomatoes
- 400g can chickpeas, drained
- ½ tsp dried chilli flakes
- 2 tbsp mild curry paste
- 100g/4oz baby leaf spinach
- 2 tbsp chopped coriander leaves
- 4 plain chapattis (Indian flatbreads)
- 4 tbsp fat-free Greek yogurt

1 Cook the sweet potatoes in salted boiling water for 10–12 minutes until tender. Meanwhile, put the tomatoes, chickpeas, chilli flakes and curry paste in another pan, and simmer gently for about 5 minutes, stirring all the time.
2 Heat grill to high. Drain the sweet potatoes and add to the tomato mixture. Stir in the spinach and cook for a minute until just starting to wilt. Stir in the coriander, season to taste and keep warm.
3 Sprinkle the chapattis with a little water and grill for 20–30 seconds each side. Spoon on the vegetable filling, top with yoghurt and fold in half to serve.

PER SERVING 289 kcals, protein 12g, carbs 54g, fat 5g, sat fat none, fibre 5g, sugar none, salt 1.08g

Rösti with egg & onions

A simple potato cake makes a welcome change from toast with your fried egg.

 15 minutes   1   Easily multiplied

- 4 tsp olive oil
- ½ red or white onion, finely sliced
- 50g/2oz potato, coarsely grated
- 1 tsp wholegrain mustard
- 1 medium egg
- 2 tomatoes, sliced
- drizzle balsamic vinegar

1 Heat half the oil in a non-stick frying pan. Fry half the onion until crispy. Drain and reserve. Mix the potato with the rest of the onion, mustard and some seasoning.

2 Add the remaining oil to the pan, add the potato mixture and press into a 12cm rösti round. Fry for 8–10 minutes until golden, turning several times. Fry the egg alongside the rösti.

3 Arrange the tomatoes on a plate and drizzle with the balsamic vinegar. Serve the rösti on the tomatoes with the egg and crispy onion on top.

PER SERVING 335 kcals, protein 9g, carbs 16g, fat 27g, sat fat 4g, fibre 3g, sugar none, salt 0.53g

Tex-Mex beans on toast

· ·

This twist on the classic comfort-food combination makes a substantial, healthy weekend brunch for one, but it can easily stretch to serve two.

 25 minutes 1

- 400g can chopped tomatoes
- 2 spring onions, whites and greens separated, both finely sliced
- 2 tsp each ground cumin and mild chilli powder
- 1 tbsp brown or BBQ sauce
- 400g can black beans, drained and rinsed
- 2 slices your favourite bread
- 1 small ripe avocado
- few good squeezes lemon or lime juice
- big dollop natural yogurt

1 Tip the tomatoes, spring-onion whites, spices and brown or BBQ sauce into a pan. Bring to a simmer and bubble for 10 minutes. Stir in the beans with some seasoning and heat through for 5 minutes.

2 Meanwhile, toast the bread, then chunkily dice half the avocado and mix with a squeeze of lemon or lime juice.

3 Mash the remaining avocado over one of the pieces of toast and sandwich with the other. Sit the avocado sandwich on a plate and top with the hot chilli beans, followed by the diced avocado and a dollop of cooling yogurt. Scatter with the spring-onion greens and tuck in.

· ·
PER SERVING 598 kcals, protein 29g, carbs 72g, fat 25g, sat fat 5g, fibre 24g, sugar 19g, salt 3.1g

Souffléd avocado omelette

Tapenade is a thick purée of olives, capers, garlic and olive oil (but watch out for hidden anchovies).

 10 minutes   4

- 3 medium eggs, separated
- 1 tbsp milk
- 2 tbsp chopped flat-leaf parsley
- 2 tsp olive oil
- 2 tbsp vegetarian black-olive tapenade
- 1 small avocado, halved, stoned and sliced
- juice ½ lemon
- tomato salad, to serve (optional)

1 Put the egg whites in a large bowl and whisk to soft peaks. Put the egg yolks in a separate bowl with the milk and parsley. Season and beat together. Add a quarter of the whites to the yolks and gently stir. Fold in the remaining egg whites.

2 Heat grill to high. Heat the oil in a 20cm non-stick frying pan. Add the egg mixture and cook for 2–3 minutes until lightly set. Put under the grill for 1–2 minutes to cook the top.

3 Spoon the olive tapenade over one half of the omelette. Top with the avocado and squeeze over the lemon juice. Fold over the other half, transfer to a plate and serve with a tomato salad, if liked.

PER SERVING 717 kcals, protein 21g, carbs 21g, fat 70g, sat fat 12g, fibre 4g, sugar none, salt 2.39g

Lentil & sweet-potato curry

This curry is comforting while still being superhealthy. It's low in fat, high in fibre, a good source of iron and also provides three of your 5-a-day.

 35 minutes 2

- 2 tbsp vegetable or olive oil
- 1 red onion, chopped
- 1 tsp each cumin and mustard seeds (any colour)
- 1 tbsp medium curry powder
- 100g/4oz red split or green lentils, or a mixture
- 2 medium sweet potatoes, peeled and cut into chunks
- 500ml/18floz vegetable stock
- 400g can chopped tomatoes
- 400g can chickpeas, drained and rinsed
- ¼ small pack coriander, leaves picked, to garnish (optional)
- natural yogurt and naan bread, to serve

1 Heat the oil in a large pan, add the onion and cook for a few minutes until softened. Add the spices and cook for 1 minute more, then stir in the lentils, sweet potatoes, stock and chopped tomatoes.

2 Bring to the boil, then cover and simmer for 20 minutes until the lentils and sweet potatoes are tender. Add the chickpeas, then heat through.

3 Season, sprinkle with coriander, if you like, and serve with seasoned yogurt and naan bread.

PER SERVING 613 kcals, protein 27g, carbs 91g, fat 18g, sat fat 2g, fibre 16g, sugar 21g, salt 1.8g

Smoky sweet-potato & bean cakes with citrus salad

. . . .

These thrifty patties count as four of your 5-a-day. Serve them as they are, or as a veggie burger in a bun with sweet-potato chips on the side.

 30-35 minutes 2

- 1 sweet potato (about 200g/8oz), cut into cubes
- 400g can red kidney beans, drained and rinsed
- 3 spring onions, finely sliced
- small bunch coriander, chopped
- 1 tbsp chipotle paste
- 2 tbsp sunflower oil
- 2 tbsp mayonnaise
- juice 1 lime
- 1 Little Gem lettuce, torn
- ½ cucumber, halved lengthways and sliced on the diagonal
- 1 carrot, halved lengthways and sliced on the diagonal

1 Microwave the sweet potato on High for 6 minutes until tender. Lightly mash the beans, then add the sweet potato, 2 of the spring onions, the coriander, chipotle paste and some seasoning. Mash a little more until the sweet potato is combined then shape into four cakes.

2 Heat the oil in a non-stick frying pan, then fry the bean cakes for 4–5 minutes each side.

3 Meanwhile, mix the mayo, lime juice and some seasoning in a bowl. Add the remaining spring onion and the salad ingredients, and toss well. Serve the citrus salad alongside the bean cakes.

. . . .

PER SERVING 431 kcals, protein 24g, carbs 39g, fat 24g, sat fat 3g, fibre 10g, sugar 15g, salt 1.4g

Stuffed mushroom bruschettas

The big mushrooms cook to a moist firmness under their cloak of peppers and melting goat's cheese.

 40 minutes   2

- 4 thick slices country-style loaf, white or brown
- 2 x 20g tubs garlic butter or 50g/2oz softened butter beaten with 1 chopped garlic clove
- 4 large flat mushrooms
- olive oil, for drizzling
- 200g jar roasted red peppers, either strips in oil or whole peppers in brine
- 140g/5oz firm goat's cheese
- mixed salad, to serve

1 Heat oven to 190C/170C fan/gas 5. Spread both sides of each slice of bread with garlic butter (no need to remove the crusts). Put the bread slices in one layer on a baking sheet.

2 Put a mushroom on top of each and drizzle with a little olive oil. Season. Drain the peppers, slice if necessary, and divide among the mushrooms.

3 Cut the goat's cheese into four slices and put one slice on top of each stack. Bake for 25–30 minutes, until the mushrooms are cooked and the cheese golden. Serve with a mixed salad.

PER SERVING 679 kcals, protein 27g, carbs 45g, fat 45g, sat fat 27g, fibre 5g, sugar none, salt 2.9g

Spicy Moroccan eggs

This quick, spicy brunch dish is cleverly made in one pan. It's packed with healthy courgettes, chickpeas, tomatoes and spinach, and flavoured with rose harissa.

 25–30 minutes   4

- 2 tsp rapeseed oil
- 1 large onion, halved and thinly sliced
- 3 garlic cloves, sliced
- 1 tbsp rose harissa paste
- 1 tsp ground coriander
- 150ml/¼ pint vegetable stock
- 400g can chickpeas, not drained
- 2 x 400g cans cherry tomatoes
- 2 courgettes, finely diced
- 200g bag baby leaf spinach
- 4 tbsp chopped coriander
- 4 eggs

1 Heat the oil in a large, deep frying pan and fry the onion and garlic for about 8 minutes, stirring every now and then, until starting to turn golden. Add the harissa and ground coriander, stir well, then pour in the stock and chickpeas with their liquid. Cover and simmer for 5 minutes, then mash about one-third of the chickpeas to thicken the stock a little.

2 Tip the tomatoes and courgettes into the pan, and cook gently for 10 minutes until the courgettes are tender. Fold in the spinach so that it wilts into the pan.

3 Stir in the chopped coriander, then make four hollows in the mixture and break in the eggs. Cover and cook for 2 minutes, then take off the heat and allow to settle for 2 minutes before serving.

PER SERVING 242 kcals, protein 16g, carbs 22g, fat 10g, sat fat 2g, fibre 8g, sugar 11g, salt 1g

Cheese & chutney melts

This dish is perfect for easy entertaining on nights at home with friends.

 30 minutes 4

- 4 large crusty bread rolls
- 2 tbsp olive oil
- 4 tbsp green tomato chutney
- 4 small rinded goat's cheeses
- 4 thyme sprigs
- green salad, to serve (optional)

1 Heat oven to 190C/170C fan/gas 5. Cut a deep hollow in the top of each roll. Remove and discard the bread from the centre and brush the insides with the oil. Season. Put on a baking sheet and bake for 5 minutes until lightly crisped.

2 Spoon the chutney into the rolls. Remove the rind from the top and bottom of each cheese and put one in each of the rolls. Push a sprig of thyme into the top and season with black pepper.

3 Scrunch foil around the roll, leaving the cheese uncovered. Bake for 15–20 minutes, until the cheese is golden and bubbling, removing the foil for the last 5 minutes. Serve with a green salad, if liked.

PER SERVING 399 kcals, protein 15g, carbs 45g, fat 19g, sat fat 7g, fibre 1g, sugar 3g, salt 1.68g

Herby stuffed mushrooms

Remember that mushrooms shrink during cooking. You could use medium mushrooms and serve more.

 30 minutes 4

- 4 very large flat mushrooms
- 2 tbsp olive oil

FOR THE STUFFING
- 3 thyme sprigs
- 4 tbsp chopped flat-leaf parsley
- 100g/4oz roasted shelled pistachio nuts, chopped
- 85g/3oz pitted black olives, chopped
- finely grated zest and juice ½ lemon
- 100g/4oz white breadcrumbs
- 140g/5oz feta, cut into small cubes
- toasted crusty bread and green salad, to serve (optional)

1 Heat oven to 200C/180C fan/gas 6. Remove the mushroom stalks and chop roughly. Brush the mushrooms with a little of the olive oil. Put in a roasting tin and season. Bake for 10 minutes until beginning to soften.
2 Meanwhile, mix all the stuffing ingredients with the chopped mushroom stalks and the remaining olive oil. Season.
3 Spoon the stuffing on top of the mushrooms and bake for a further 5–8 minutes, until the feta begins to soften. Serve immediately on toasted crusty bread with a green salad, if liked.

Bhaji frittata

. . . .

This frittata tastes as good cold as it does warm, making it ideal for a packed lunch or to take on a picnic.

 40 minutes   4

- 2 tbsp vegetable oil
- 2 onions, thinly sliced
- 1 garlic clove, finely chopped
- 2 tsp mild curry powder
- 450g/1lb potatoes, coarsely grated and any excess liquid squeezed out
- 6 medium eggs, beaten
- 100g/4oz frozen peas
- small pack coriander, roughly chopped
- mango chutney, natural yogurt and naan bread, to serve (optional)

1 Heat oven to 200C/180C fan/gas 6. Heat the oil in an ovenproof frying pan and fry the onions for about 10 minutes over a medium heat until golden. Add the garlic and curry powder, and cook for 1–2 minutes.

2 Next, add the grated potatoes to the pan and cook for 5–8 minutes, stirring occasionally. You want the potatoes not only to soften but also to catch a little and turn golden in patches. Season the eggs, then pour into the pan with the peas and most of the coriander, swirling to coat the potato mixture. Cook for 1 minute more, then transfer to the oven for 10 minutes until the eggs have set. Sprinkle with the remaining coriander and serve with mango chutney, natural yogurt and naan bread, if you like.

. . . .
PER SERVING 282 kcals, protein 13g, carbs 27g, fat 14g, sat fat 3g, fibre 6g, sugar 5g, salt 0.3g

Mushroom & pepper melts

. . . .

This indulgent meal for one can be easily increased to serve as many as you need it to.

 30 minutes 1  Easily multiplied

- 1 tbsp olive oil
- ½ red pepper, deseeded and sliced
- 1 Portobello mushroom, thickly sliced
- 1 garlic clove, finely chopped
- 1 tsp thyme leaves
- 1–2 slices crusty bread
- 75g/2½oz Camembert or Brie, sliced

1 Heat grill to high. Put the oil, pepper, mushroom, garlic and thyme leaves in a bowl. Season well, then toss together.

2 Heat a griddle pan over a high heat and cook the pepper and mushroom slices for 10–12 minutes, turning every so often, until softened and charred.

3 Meanwhile, toast the bread on one side until golden. Pile the griddled veg and any of the remaining flavoured oil from the bowl on to the untoasted side of the bread. Top with the cheese and grill for 3–5 minutes until bubbling and golden.

. . . .

PER MELT 431 kcals, protein 21g, carbs 20g, fat 29g, sat fat 12g, fibre 4g, sugar 8g, salt 1.5g

Stilton & walnut tart

· ·

This tart can stretch to feed extra people with the addition of a big mixed salad and garlic bread.

 45 minutes   6

- 600g/1lb 5oz onions
- 3 tbsp olive oil
- 1 tbsp balsamic vinegar
- 375g pack ready-rolled puff pastry
- 175g/6oz Stilton
- 50g pack walnut pieces

1 Heat oven to 200C/180C fan/gas 6. Peel the onions and thinly slice them. Heat the oil in a large frying pan, add the onions and fry until softened and lightly browned, stirring occasionally. This will take about 10 minutes.

2 Splash in the vinegar, season, then cook for a further 5 minutes, until lightly caramelised. Leave to cool while you unroll the pastry and use to line a 23 x 33cm shallow oblong tin.

3 Spread the onions over the pastry, then crumble the Stilton on top and scatter with walnuts. Bake for 15–20 minutes, until the pastry is crisp and golden and the cheese has melted. Cool for 5 minutes before serving, cut into squares to serve.

· ·

PER SERVING 446 kcals, protein 13g, carbs 31g, fat 31g, sat fat 7g, fibre 2g, sugar none, salt 1.19g

Fattoush

· ·

Serve this classic crunchy, light Middle Eastern salad as part of a bigger meal or a
lunchbox filler.

 15 minutes   2

FOR THE SALAD
- 2 tomatoes, chopped into chunks
- ¼ cucumber, deseeded and sliced
- ½ red onion, sliced
- 1 small head romaine lettuce, shredded
- handful mint leaves, roughly chopped
- handful parsley leaves, roughly chopped
- 2 pitta breads
- 1 tsp ground sumac

FOR THE DRESSING
- ½ garlic clove, crushed
- 2 tbsp red wine vinegar
- 1 tbsp extra virgin olive oil
- juice ½ lemon

1 Toss together all the salad ingredients except for the pitta bread and sumac. Combine all the dressing ingredients.
2 Toast the pitta breads until lightly golden and crisp. When cool, tear into pieces and combine with the salad and dressing. Spoon into bowls or plastic boxes and sprinkle over the sumac.

· ·
PER SERVING 358 kcals, protein 12g, carbs 57g, fat 18g, sat fat 1g, fibre 6g, sugar 10g, salt 1.1g

Spaghetti Genovese

Quick and tasty and cooked in one pan so there's hardly any washing-up.

 20 minutes 4

- 300g/10oz new potatoes, sliced
- 300g/10oz spaghetti
- 200g/8oz trimmed green beans, cut in half
- 120g carton fresh pesto
- olive oil, for drizzling

1 Pour boiling water into a very large pan until half full. Return to the boil, then add the potatoes and spaghetti, and a little salt.
2 Cook for 10 minutes until the potatoes and pasta are almost tender. Tip in the green beans and cook for 5 minutes more.
3 Drain well, reserving 4 tablespoons of the cooking liquid. Return the potatoes, pasta and beans to the pan, then stir in the fresh pesto and reserved cooking liquid. Season to taste, divide among four serving plates and drizzle with a little olive oil.

PER SERVING 330 kcals, protein 23g, carbs 8g, fat 23g, sat fat 9g, fibre trace, sugar 7g, salt 0.5g

Pasta with flageolet beans

A simple sauce based on a can of beans from the storecupboard, plus wine and cream for richness.

 40 minutes 4

- 2 tbsp olive oil
- 2 small red onions, cut into thick wedges
- 4 garlic cloves, roughly chopped
- 400g can flageolet beans, drained and rinsed
- 1 tbsp chopped rosemary
- 150ml/¼ pint vegetable stock
- 150ml/¼ pint white wine
- 4 tbsp double cream
- 100g/4oz green beans
- 350g/12oz pappardelle (broad pasta ribbons)

1 Heat the oil in large pan, add the onions and cook until softened. Add the garlic, flageolet beans, rosemary, stock and wine, and simmer for 10 minutes.

2 Season, add the cream and simmer for a further 5 minutes. Meanwhile, bring a pan of lightly salted water to the boil. Add the green beans and cook for 5 minutes until tender. Remove with a slotted spoon and keep hot.

3 Add the pasta to the boiling water and cook according to the pack instructions. Drain and toss with the creamy sauce. Divide among four bowls and serve topped with the green beans.

PER SERVING 582 kcals, protein 21g, carbs 85g, fat 18g, sat fat 6g, fibre 9g, sugar none, salt 0.95g

Roasted-pepper linguine with crisp crumbs

You can extend this recipe to use other summer vegetables like chunks of courgette or whole cherry tomatoes – simply toss them in oil and roast alongside the peppers.

 45 minutes   4

- 4 mixed peppers, deseeded and sliced
- 2 tbsp olive oil
- 2 garlic cloves, finely sliced
- pinch chilli flakes
- 100g/4oz fresh white bread, whizzed to crumbs
- 300g/10oz linguine
- 85g/3oz pitted green olives, halved
- ½ small pack basil, torn, saving a few small leaves to garnish
- zest ½ lemon
- 25g/1oz butter

1 Heat oven to 200C/180C fan/gas 6. Put the peppers in a roasting tin and toss in half the oil. Season and spread into a single layer. Roast for 30 minutes or until tender.

2 Add the remaining oil to a frying pan then tip in the garlic and soften over a low heat for 10 seconds. Add the chilli flakes, breadcrumbs and some seasoning, and toast until golden brown and crisp then tip on to a plate.

3 Cook the pasta according to the pack instructions, then drain – reserving a few tablespoons of cooking water. Toss together with the roasted peppers, olives, torn basil, lemon zest, reserved cooking water, butter and some seasoning. Sprinkle with the crisp crumbs and reserved basil leaves, and serve.

PER SERVING 437 kcals, protein 13g, carbs 59g, fat 17g, sat fat 5g, fibre 4g, sugar 11g, salt 1.3g

Spicy cauliflower pasta

Chilli, lemon, pine nuts and sultanas make bland pasta and cauliflower surprisingly tasty.

 20 minutes 4

- 1 medium cauliflower, cut into small florets
- 350g/12oz trompetti or other pasta tubes
- 4 tbsp olive oil
- 2 garlic cloves, sliced
- 1 red chilli, deseeded and sliced
- 85g/3oz pine nuts
- 50g/2oz sultanas
- finely pared zest 1 lemon, shredded (or use a zester)
- juice ½ lemon
- 4 tbsp chopped flat-leaf parsley leaves
- 50g/2oz vegetarian Parmesan, grated (optional)

1 Cook the cauliflower in salted boiling water for 2 minutes. Drain and rinse with cold water to stop it cooking further. Cook the pasta in salted boiling water according to the pack instructions.

2 Meanwhile, heat the oil in a large frying pan. Add the cauliflower and fry for 3 minutes until lightly golden. Reduce the heat, add the garlic, chilli and pine nuts, and cook for a further 2 minutes.

3 Add the drained pasta, the sultanas, lemon zest and juice and parsley to the cauliflower mix. Season and toss together with the Parmesan, if using.

PER SERVING 691 kcals, protein 22g, carbs 78g, fat 35g, sat fat 6g, fibre 5g, sugar none, salt 0.42g

Peanut noodles with coriander-omelette ribbons

. . . .

The coriander-omelette ribbons would also be great as the 'egg' element through a veggie-fried rice dish.

 30 minutes 4

- 250g pack medium egg noodles
- 2 tsp sesame oil, plus a little extra for drizzling
- 1½ tbsp sunflower oil
- 3 carrots, cut into thin batons
- 2 garlic cloves, finely sliced
- ½ Chinese cabbage, roughly sliced
- 5 spring onions, thinly sliced on the diagonal
- 2 tbsp crunchy peanut butter
- 2 tsp light soy sauce
- 1 tbsp sweet chilli sauce
- 3 eggs, beaten
- handful coriander leaves, roughly chopped, plus a few sprigs to garnish

1 Cook the noodles according to the pack instructions. Drain, reserving 2 tablespoons of the cooking water. Toss the noodles in a drizzle of sesame oil.

2 Heat half the sunflower oil in a wok. Add the carrots and stir-fry until tender. Tip in the garlic, cabbage and half the spring onions, and stir-fry for 1–2 minutes until the cabbage begins to wilt. Mix together the peanut butter, soy, 2 teaspoons sesame oil, chilli sauce and reserved cooking water, and add to the pan. Toss in the noodles and heat until warmed.

3 Whisk the eggs, chopped coriander and some seasoning in a bowl. Heat the remaining sunflower oil in a non-stick frying pan. Tip in the eggs, stir once, then allow to set on one side. Turn over carefully and cook the other side until set and golden. Slide on to a board. Cool for 1 minute, then cut into strips and scatter over the noodles, along with the remaining spring onions and coriander sprigs.

. . . .
PER SERVING 453 kcals, protein 16g, carbs 51g, fat 20g, sat fat 4g, fibre 7g, sugar 10g, salt 1.3g

Ravioli with pumpkin

Pumpkin can be bland, but here it's spiced up with chilli, sage and lemon zest.

 30 minutes 4

- 500g/1lb 2oz pack fresh cheese ravioli
- 1 tbsp olive oil
- 1 onion, finely chopped
- 1 garlic clove, crushed
- 425g can solid-pack pumpkin
- 50g/2oz vegetarian Parmesan, finely grated
- pinch crushed chilli flakes
- finely grated zest 1 lemon
- 25g/1oz butter
- 85g/3oz fresh white breadcrumbs
- 2 tbsp chopped sage leaves
- deep-fried sage leaves, to garnish (optional)

1 Cook the ravioli according to the pack instructions. Meanwhile, heat the olive oil in a small pan, and fry the onion and garlic for 2–3 minutes, until softened. Add the pumpkin, 300ml/½ pint water, the grated Parmesan, chilli flakes and lemon zest. Stir well and cook over a low heat for 3–4 minutes. Season.

2 In a small frying pan, melt the butter, then stir in the breadcrumbs and fry until lightly golden. Stir in the chopped sage.

3 Drain the ravioli and spoon into bowls. Pour over the pumpkin sauce and sprinkle with the toasted sage breadcrumbs. Serve with the deep-fried sage, if liked.

Roasted squash, shallot, spinach & ricotta pasta

· ·

This quick supper is made healthy by using wholemeal pasta. Any leftovers can be served as a salad the following day – just dress with an extra drizzle of olive oil.

 40 minutes · 4

- 1 butternut squash (about 800g/1lb 12oz), peeled and diced
- 4 banana shallots, quartered lengthways (roots intact)
- 2 tbsp olive oil
- 400g/14oz wholemeal pasta shapes
- 300g/10oz baby leaf spinach
- 6 tbsp ricotta
- 4 sage leaves, very finely chopped
- zest and juice 1 lemon
- a few gratings nutmeg

1 Heat oven to 200C/180C fan/gas 6. Tip the squash and shallots into a large roasting dish. Toss in the oil, season and roast for 40 minutes, stirring once.

2 Meanwhile, cook the pasta according to the pack instructions, reserving a few tablespoons of cooking water. Put the spinach in a large colander and pour over boiling water to wilt. Allow to cool a little, then squeeze out as much excess water as possible. Pop into a bowl with two-thirds of the ricotta, the sage, lemon juice and zest, nutmeg and some seasoning, then stir.

3 Next, tip the ricotta mixture into the hot drained pasta. Stir, adding the reserved cooking water. Mix most of the roasted veg with the pasta. Divide into bowls and dot with the remaining ricotta and scatter over any final bits of roast veg to serve.

· ·

PER SERVING 504 kcals, protein 18g, carbs 84g, fat 11g, sat fat 3g, fibre 14g, sugar 14g, salt 0.4g

Cheese & tomato cannelloni

· · · · · · · · · · · · · · · · · · · ·

Using fresh pasta in this dish means there's no pre-cooking needed.

 1 hour 20 minutes   4

- 5 tbsp fruity olive oil, plus extra for greasing
- 750g/1lb 10oz ripe cherry tomatoes
- 2 tsp dried oregano
- 2 tsp golden caster sugar
- 6 tbsp fresh red or green pesto
- 200g/8oz soft rindless goat's cheese
- 12 fresh lasagne sheets
- 350g/12oz ripe vine tomatoes, thinly sliced
- 3 tbsp freshly grated Parmesan
- few basil leaves, to garnish
- green salad, to serve

1 Heat oven to 220C/200C fan/gas 7. Oil a shallow baking dish. Halve 250g/9oz of the cherry tomatoes. Heat the oil in a frying pan, add the whole cherry tomatoes, cover and cook over a high heat, shaking the pan, for 5 minutes. Add the oregano and sugar. Season well.

2 Beat the pesto into the goat's cheese. Lay out the lasagne and spread the cheese mixture over each sheet. Top with vine-tomato slices and roll up like a Swiss roll. Spoon half the cherry-tomato sauce into the dish. Arrange the pasta rolls on top and spoon over any remaining tomato sauce. Scatter the cherry-tomato halves on top and cover with foil.

3 Bake for 25–30 minutes. Uncover, sprinkle with the cheese and bake for 10 minutes until brown. Serve with basil leaves to garnish and a green salad.

· ·

PER SERVING 635 kcals, protein 21g, carbs 57g, fat 37g, sat fat 5g, fibre 6g, sugar 3g, salt 1.46g

Fiorentina baked pasta

This pasta dish is perfect to have bubbling in the oven while you chat to your guests.

 1 hour 4

- 1 tbsp olive oil
- 500g/1lb 2oz chestnut mushrooms, halved
- 2 garlic cloves, chopped
- 300g carton fresh spinach and cheese sauce
- 300ml/½ pint milk
- 50g/2oz vegetarian Parmesan, grated
- 300g/10oz puntalette (rice-shaped pasta)

1 Heat oven to 190C/170C fan/gas 5. Heat the oil in a large frying pan, add the mushrooms and cook over a high heat for 5 minutes until lightly golden. Reduce the heat, add the garlic and cook for 2 minutes. Season and put in a shallow 1.5 litre ovenproof dish.

2 Put the spinach and cheese sauce, milk, half the Parmesan and the pasta in a large bowl. Stir and season to taste. Pour the sauce over the mushrooms and scatter over the remaining Parmesan.

3 Bake for 45 minutes until the pasta is tender and most of the liquid has been absorbed.

PER SERVING 594 kcals, protein 27g, carbs 67g, fat 26g, sat fat 12g, fibre 4g, sugar none, salt 1.56g

Gnocchi with broad beans

Potato gnocchi, bought vacuum-packed, make a great fridge or freezer standby.

 20 minutes   4

- 350g pack potato gnocchi
- 2 tbsp olive oil
- 250g/9oz small cup mushrooms, halved
- 2 garlic cloves, crushed
- 200g/8oz frozen baby broad beans
- 3 tbsp chopped tarragon leaves
- 250g tub mascarpone cheese
- 1 tbsp lemon juice
- vegetarian Parmesan shavings and pared lemon zest, to garnish
- salad leaves, to serve (optional)

1 Cook the gnocchi according to the pack instructions. Drain into a medium bowl. Heat the oil in a frying pan, add the mushrooms and fry quickly over a high heat until browned. Lift out with a slotted spoon and add to the gnocchi.

2 Wipe out the pan then add the garlic, beans, tarragon and mascarpone. Heat gently, stirring, until the mascarpone has melted. Add the lemon juice, mushrooms and gnocchi to the frying pan. Heat through for 1 minute. Season to taste.

3 Divide among serving plates and scatter over the Parmesan shavings and pared lemon zest. Serve with salad leaves, if liked.

PER SERVING 488 kcals, protein 10g, carbs 28g, fat 38g, sat fat 20g, fibre 5g, sugar none, salt 0.54g

Leek & mushroom risotto

· ·

This delicious veggie risotto is cooked in the microwave, which cuts down the need for stirring.

 40 minutes 4

- 25g/1oz butter
- 1 tbsp olive oil
- 1 leek, cut into thin slices
- 1 garlic clove, crushed
- 300g/10oz risotto rice
- 850ml/1½ pints hot vegetable stock
- 250g/9oz chestnut mushrooms, sliced
- 50g/2oz Parmesan, grated
- green salad, to serve

1 Put the butter, oil, leek and garlic into a large bowl. Cover with cling film and cook on High for 5 minutes.

2 Stir the rice into the hot leeks, then stir in the stock and season. Cook, uncovered, on High for 10 minutes. Throw in the mushrooms, stir and cook on High for 6 minutes.

3 Mix in half the Parmesan and leave the risotto to stand for 5 minutes. Serve with a green salad and the remaining Parmesan for sprinkling.

· ·
PER SERVING 397 kcals, protein 13g, carbs 60g, fat 13g, sat fat 6g, fibre 3g, sugar none, salt 1.22g

Ravioli with artichokes, leek & lemon

This supper for two makes clever use of quick-cook fresh ravioli, and the artichokes will work with whichever filling you choose.

 20 minutes   2

- 280g jar artichoke antipasto, drained, reserving 1 tbsp oil, artichokes roughly chopped
- 1 large leek, finely sliced
- 1 garlic clove, crushed
- 3 tbsp soft cheese
- zest and juice 1 lemon
- 250g pack spinach and ricotta ravioli, or your favourite filling
- 2 large handfuls rocket leaves and grated vegetarian Parmesan, to garnish (optional)

1 Heat the reserved oil from the artichokes in a large pan, then add the leek and garlic. Fry for 5 minutes over a medium heat until the leek is soft. Stir in the artichokes, soft cheese and lemon zest, then heat through. Season to taste and add a squeeze of lemon juice.

2 Meanwhile, cook the ravioli according to the pack instructions. Drain, add to the pan with the artichokes and soft cheese, and toss through. Serve topped with the rocket and a grating of Parmesan, if you like.

PER SERVING 513 kcals, protein 16g, carbs 43g, fat 31g, sat fat 13g, fibre 9g, sugar 7g, salt 3.5g

Easy pesto lasagne

· ·

Children love lasagne, and this one will encourage them to eat their greens. It also cleverly uses mascarpone cheese, so you don't have to make a white sauce.

 55 minutes   4-6

- 190g jar green pesto
- 500g tub mascarpone
- 200g bag spinach leaves, roughly chopped
- 250g/9oz frozen peas
- small pack each basil and mint, leaves chopped, a few basil leaves reserved to garnish
- 12 fresh lasagne sheets
- splash milk
- 85g/3oz Parmesan (or vegetarian alternative), grated
- 50g/2oz pine nuts
- green salad, to serve (optional)

1 Heat oven to 180C/160C fan/gas 4. Put the pesto, half the mascarpone and 250ml/9fl oz water (or vegetable stock, if you have some) in a pan. Heat and mix until smooth and bubbling. Add the spinach and peas, and cook for a few more minutes until the spinach has wilted and the peas have thawed. Add the herbs and season.

2 Put a third of the pesto mixture into a baking dish roughly 18 x 25cm. Top with 4 of the lasagne sheets, then repeat with two more layers of sauce and lasagne sheets, finishing with a layer of pasta. Mix enough milk into the remaining mascarpone to make a white-sauce consistency, season, then pour over the top. Sprinkle with the Parmesan and pine nuts. Bake for 35–40 minutes until golden brown on top and bubbling around the edges.

3 Scatter over the reserved basil leaves and serve with a green salad, if you like.

· ·

PER SERVING (6) 787 kcals, protein 21g, carbs 27g, fat 62g, sat fat 30g, fibre 6g, sugar 7g, salt 1.5g

Spicy nasi goreng

You could use leftover rice to make this tasty and colourful Indonesian fried-rice mixture, if it has been kept well chilled.

 35 minutes   2

- 300g/10oz long grain rice, rinsed
- 2 medium eggs, beaten
- 3 garlic cloves
- 2 red chillies, thinly sliced
- 2 onions, sliced
- 3 tbsp groundnut oil
- 1 yellow pepper, deseeded and sliced
- 2 carrots, cut into matchsticks
- 2 tbsp dark soy sauce
- 4 spring onions, shredded
- 4 tbsp chopped coriander

1 Put the rice in a wok, add 600ml/1 pint water and bring to the boil. Cover and cook over a very low heat for 15 minutes, until all the liquid has been absorbed. Tip into a shallow dish and leave to cool.

2 Meanwhile, heat the wok. Add the eggs and cook, stirring, until scrambled. Remove to a bowl. Whizz the garlic, half the chilli and half the onions to a paste in a blender. Heat the oil in the wok and fry the paste for 1 minute. Add the rest of the onion and chilli, plus the vegetables, and stir-fry for 2 minutes.

3 Add the cold rice and stir-fry for 3 minutes. Stir in the soy sauce, spring onions, coriander and eggs, and fry until piping hot. Season and serve straight away.

PER SERVING 445 kcals, protein 10g, carbs 72g, fat 15g, sat fat 3g, fibre 2g, sugar none, salt 0.16g

Spaghetti with fresh tomato sauce

It's worth trying to get hold of burrata – a creamier relative of mozzarella. It will go oozingly melty and create a sauce that clings to the pasta.

 10 minutes 2

- 200g/8oz spaghetti or linguine
- 1 red chilli, deseeded and finely chopped
- 2 shallots, finely chopped
- 1 tbsp extra virgin olive oil
- zest 1 lemon
- 1 tbsp red wine vinegar
- 2 tsp caster sugar
- 300g/10oz tomatoes, diced
- 125g ball mozzarella or burrata, torn into pieces
- handful basil leaves, torn, to garnish

1 Cook the pasta according to the pack instructions.
2 Meanwhile, put the chilli, shallots, oil, lemon zest, vinegar, sugar and tomatoes into a big mortar. If yours isn't big enough, put it all in a bowl and just use the pestle in that. Add a good amount of sea salt and freshly ground black pepper, and bash everything together.
3 Drain the pasta and toss together with the tomato mixture and cheese. Scatter over the basil and serve immediately.

PER SERVING 598 kcals, protein 25g, carbs 78g, fat 21g, sat fat 10g, fibre 5g, sugar 12g, salt 0.7g

Tofu chow mein

Tofu is bean curd. It tastes bland but, like chicken, it is good at absorbing flavours from other ingredients.

 25 minutes   4

- 250g pack egg noodles
- 1 tbsp vegetable oil
- 3 spring onions, sliced
- 2 garlic cloves, finely chopped
- 2cm/¾in knob ginger, peeled and finely chopped
- 285g pack firm tofu, cut into small cubes
- 227g can bamboo shoots, drained, rinsed and sliced
- 100g/4oz beansprouts
- 100g/4oz mangetout, sliced lengthways
- 2 tbsp soy sauce
- 2 tbsp sweet chilli sauce

1 Cook the noodles according to the pack instructions. Meanwhile, heat the oil in a large frying pan or wok and stir-fry the spring onions, garlic and ginger for 1–2 minutes, until slightly softened.

2 Add the tofu cubes to the spring-onion mix and fry over a high heat for 2–3 minutes until golden. Stir in the bamboo shoots, beansprouts and mangetout, and stir-fry for a further 1–2 minutes.

3 Drain the noodles and add to the vegetables with the soy sauce and chilli sauce. Toss together and serve immediately.

PER SERVING 361 kcals, protein 16g, carbs 49g, fat 12g, sat fat 1g, fibre 4g, sugar none, salt 1.4g

Baked asparagus risotto

Cooking a risotto in the oven saves you laborious stirring time, plus this one's low in fat and calories, and cleverly uses a tin of soup as its base.

 55 minutes   4

- 2 tsp olive oil
- 1 small onion, chopped
- 300g/10oz risotto rice
- 400ml can asparagus soup
- 850ml/1½ pints vegetable stock
- small bunch flat-leaf parsley, chopped
- 300g/10oz asparagus spears, ends trimmed
- 10 cherry tomatoes, halved
- 25g/1oz Parmesan (or vegetarian alternative), grated

1 Heat oven to 200C/180C fan/gas 6. Heat the oil in an ovenproof casserole dish with a lid, add the onion and cook for 5 minutes until softened. Add the rice and cook for 1 minute more, stirring to coat in the oil. Tip in the soup and stock, season and stir well to combine, then bring to the boil. Cover and bake in the oven for 15 minutes.

2 Remove the casserole dish from the oven and give the rice a good mix, stirring in the parsley. Put the asparagus and tomatoes on top of the rice. Return to the oven, uncovered, for a further 15 minutes. Scatter with the cheese to serve.

PER SERVING 403 kcals, protein 12g, carbs 70g, fat 8g, sat fat 4g, fibre 4g, sugar 6g, salt 1.3g

Lemon & mint aubergine tagine with almond couscous

This Moroccan-inspired vegetarian stew is filled with all the delicious aromatics of North Africa, and without the yogurt it's vegan friendly.

 50 minutes 4

- 1 tbsp rapeseed oil
- 1 large onion, chopped
- 3 garlic cloves, chopped
- 1 tbsp harissa paste
- 1 tsp cumin seeds
- ½ tsp ground cinnamon
- 200ml/7fl oz reduced-salt vegetable stock
- 400g can chopped tomatoes
- 350g/12oz baby aubergines
- 2 strips lemon zest, finely chopped
- 390g can butter beans, drained
- 175g/6oz wholemeal couscous
- 40g/1½oz toasted flaked almonds
- 150g pot 0% fat probiotic natural yogurt, mixed with ½ crushed garlic clove and 2 tbsp chopped mint, plus leaves to garnish (optional)

1 Heat the oil in a large non-stick pan with a lid and fry the onion and garlic for 5 minutes. Stir in the harissa, cumin and cinnamon, cook briefly, then tip in the stock and tomatoes.

2 Trim the aubergines and slit a couple of times then add to the pan with the lemon zest. Cover the pan and cook gently for 15–20 minutes until the aubergines are meltingly tender. Add the butter beans and warm through.

3 Meanwhile, cook the couscous according to the pack instructions, then stir in the almonds. Serve the aubergine tagine on the couscous with the garlic–mint yogurt drizzled over, and a garnish of mint leaves, if you like.

PER SERVING 361 kcals, protein 16g, carbs 50g, fat 10g, sat fat 1g, fibre 9g, sugar 12g, salt 0.9g

Halloumi & pepper kebabs with lemony cabbage salad

· ·

The Cypriot cheese halloumi is a great choice for meat-free kebabs as it doesn't melt and stays firmly on the skewers as the kebabs cook.

 40 minutes   4

- 500g/1lb 2oz halloumi, cut into cubes
- 3 red peppers, deseeded and cut into squares
- 1 tbsp olive oil
- 1 tsp oregano (fresh or dried)
- pitta breads and tzatziki, to serve

FOR THE SALAD
- 500g/1lb 2oz red cabbage, finely shredded
- 2 tbsp extra virgin olive oil
- juice ½ lemon
- handful flat-leaf parsley, finely shredded

1 Thread the halloumi and red peppers on to eight soaked wooden skewers and put on a plate. Stir the oil and oregano together, then drizzle it over the kebabs. Season well with black pepper – you shouldn't need salt.
2 To make the salad, put the cabbage in a bowl. Mix together the oil, lemon juice and some seasoning. Pour this dressing over the cabbage, toss until well coated, then stir through the parsley.
3 Barbecue the skewers or cook under a preheated hot grill for 10 minutes on each side until the cheese is golden and the peppers slightly charred. Serve on a large platter with pitta breads and tzatziki, with the salad on the side.

· ·
PER SERVING 546 kcals, protein 29g, carbs 13g, fat 42g, sat fat 22g, fibre 5g, sugar 12g, salt 3.9g

South Indian egg curry

This aromatic tomato-based curry is even better when it is made a day or two ahead and reheated, but don't freeze it or the eggs will go rubbery.

 50 minutes   4

- 4 tbsp vegetable oil
- 1½ tsp mustard seeds
- 1½ tbsp curry leaves
- 2 large red onions, chopped
- 50g/2oz piece ginger, peeled and finely chopped
- 1 tsp turmeric powder
- ½ tsp chilli powder
- 2 x 400g cans chopped tomatoes
- 1–2 tsp sugar
- 8 eggs
- small bunch coriander, chopped
- mango chutney, natural yogurt, naan bread and cooked basmati rice, to serve (optional)

1 Heat the oil in a wok or shallow pan, then toss in the mustard seeds followed by the curry leaves. Once the leaves have stopped spluttering, reduce the heat and add the onions and ginger. Fry over a medium heat for about 10 minutes until golden.

2 Stir in the turmeric and chilli powder, and cook for a few more seconds. Tip in the tomatoes and sugar. Simmer, uncovered, for 10–15 minutes until thickened, adding a splash of water if needed.

3 Meanwhile, boil the eggs for 8 minutes, then cool under cold running water before peeling and halving. Add to the curry, cover with a tight-fitting lid and simmer for a few minutes. Stir the coriander into the curry and serve with mango chutney, yogurt, rice and naan, if you like.

PER SERVING 317 kcals, protein 16g, carbs 39g, fat 27g, sat fat 14g, fibre 3g, sugar 33g, salt 0.3g

Potato & onion tart

· ·

A filling tart, delicious served hot or cold with salads.

 50 minutes 🕑 4

- 375g pack ready-rolled shortcrust pastry, thawed if frozen
- 2 tbsp olive oil
- 450g/1lb onions, thinly sliced
- 2 garlic cloves, crushed
- 3 tbsp thyme leaves or 1 tbsp dried
- 750g/1lb 10oz floury potatoes, peeled and thickly sliced
- 2 eggs
- 200ml tub crème fraîche
- 2 tbsp wholegrain mustard
- salad leaves, to serve

1 Heat oven to 220C/200C fan/gas 7. Use the pastry to line the base and sides of a Swiss roll tin about 23 x 33cm. Heat the oil in a large frying pan and fry the onions for 8–10 minutes, until just beginning to caramelise. Stir in the garlic and most of the thyme, and cook for a further 2 minutes. Scatter half into the pastry case.

2 Parboil the potatoes in salted water for 4–5 minutes. Drain well and arrange in the case. Scatter over the remaining onions.

3 Beat together the eggs, crème fraîche and mustard. Season well and pour over the vegetables. Scatter over the rest of the thyme and bake the tart for 20 minutes, until the filling has set and is golden. Serve with a leafy salad.

· ·

PER SERVING 706 kcals, protein 14g, carbs 84g, fat 37g, sat fat 14g, fibre 6g, sugar none, salt 0.84g

Chickpea fritters with courgette salad

These pancake-style fritters are made using storecupboard ingredients then served with a warm courgette salad to make a substantial, summery main course.

 35 minutes   4

- 400g can chickpeas, drained and rinsed
- 2 eggs
- 3 tbsp full-fat milk
- 4 tbsp plain flour
- 1 tsp baking powder
- bunch spring onions, ½ chopped, ½ sliced lengthways
- 4 tsp harissa paste
- 3 tbsp sunflower oil
- 2 courgettes, thinly sliced
- 200g pack feta, crumbled
- small bunch mint leaves
- 150ml pot natural yogurt

1 Blitz half the can of chickpeas in a food processor until smooth. With the motor running, add the eggs and milk, then sift in the flour and baking powder. Process until you have a lump-free batter. Fold in the whole chickpeas and chopped spring onions. Season and add half the harissa.

2 Heat half the oil in a large frying pan and fry the courgettes in batches until golden; keep warm in a low oven. Heat a little more of the oil and cook 2 tablespoon-portions of the fritter mix in batches for a couple of minutes, until you see bubbles appear, then flip over and cook the other side until golden. Keep warm with the courgettes.

3 Toss together the courgettes, feta, mint and sliced spring onions. Divide among four plates and top each with two fritters and a dollop of yogurt swirled with the remaining harissa.

PER SERVING 406 kcals, protein 19g, carbs 28g, fat 24g, sat fat 9g, fibre 5g, sugar 4g, salt 2.6g

Indian chickpea salad

· ·

A substantial main-course salad with spiced canned chickpeas and naan bread croutons.

 30 minutes 4

- 6 tbsp olive oil
- 3 garlic cloves, sliced
- 2 red chillies, deseeded and sliced
- 4 tsp cumin seeds, lightly crushed
- 2 x 400g cans chickpeas, drained and rinsed
- 3 tomatoes, halved, deseeded and diced
- pared zest and juice 1 lemon
- 1 naan bread

FOR THE SALAD

- 25g/1oz coriander leaves
- ½ cucumber, cut into batons
- 1 medium red onion, sliced
- 100g/4oz baby leaf spinach

1 Put 5 tablespoons of the oil in a pan. Add the garlic, chillies and cumin, and warm over a medium heat for 10 minutes. Take care not to burn the garlic. Add the chickpeas and heat through for 5 minutes. Meanwhile, heat grill to high.

2 Add the tomatoes, lemon zest and juice to the chickpeas. Season. Brush the naan bread with the remaining oil and grill both sides until crisp. Tear into bite-sized pieces.

3 Toss together the salad ingredients and divide among serving plates. Spoon the chickpeas over and top with the naan-bread croutons.

· ·

PER SERVING 641 kcals, protein 23g, carbs 66g, fat 33g, sat fat 6g, fibre 11g, sugar trace, salt 0.65g

Griddled vegetable & feta tart

Crispy filo pastry makes a great base for this summery tart and has the added advantage of being lower in fat than normal pastry.

 50 minutes 4

- 2 tbsp olive oil
- 1 aubergine, sliced
- 2 courgettes, sliced
- 2 red onions, cut into chunky wedges
- 3 large sheets filo pastry
- 10–12 cherry tomatoes, halved
- drizzle balsamic vinegar
- 85g/3oz low-fat feta, crumbled
- 1 tsp dried oregano
- large bag mixed salad leaves and low-fat dressing, to serve

1 Heat oven to 220C/200C fan/gas 7. Pop a 33 x 23cm baking sheet in the oven to heat up. Brush a griddle pan with about 1 teaspoon of the oil and griddle the aubergine until nicely charred, then remove. Repeat with the courgettes and onions, using a little more oil, if you need to.

2 Remove the baking sheet from the oven and brush with a little more of the oil. Brush 1 sheet of the filo with more oil, top with another sheet, add a little more oil and repeat with the final sheet. Transfer the pastry to the hot baking sheet, carefully pushing it into the edges a little.

3 Arrange the griddled veg on top, then season. Add the tomatoes, cut-side up, then drizzle on the vinegar and any remaining oil. Crumble on the feta and sprinkle with oregano. Cook for about 20 minutes until crispy and golden. Serve with the dressed mixed salad leaves.

PER SERVING 191 kcals, protein 8g, carbs 19g, fat 9g, sat fat 3g, fibre 5g, sugar 8g, salt 0.5g

Aubergines with goat's cheese

Most melting cheeses will taste great grilled on top of aubergine slices. Try using Brie for a change.

 25 minutes 4

- 4 medium aubergines, halved lengthways
- 100ml/3½fl oz olive oil
- 2 tbsp sun-dried tomato paste
- 25g/1oz basil leaves
- 4 x 60g individual rinded goat's cheeses
- 1 tbsp white wine vinegar
- 1 tsp Dijon mustard
- pinch caster sugar
- 160g bag mixed salad leaves
- 85g/3oz radishes, halved
- crusty bread, to serve

1 Heat grill to hot. Brush both sides of the aubergine halves with 3 tablespoons of the oil and season. Put the aubergines, cut-side up, on a baking sheet and grill for 7 minutes. Turn them over and grill for a further 5 minutes, until lightly scorched.

2 Spread the cut sides of the aubergines with the tomato paste and arrange basil leaves on top. Slice each cheese into four rounds and arrange on the aubergines. Season and grill until bubbling.

3 Whisk the remaining oil, the vinegar, mustard and sugar in a salad bowl. Toss the vegetables in the dressing until coated. Divide the salad among serving plates and arrange the cheesy aubergine halves on top. Serve with crusty bread.

PER SERVING 416 kcals, protein 12g, carbs 10g, fat 37g, sat fat 4g, fibre 7g, sugar none, salt 2.36g

Sri Lankan runner-bean curry

This vegan curry is traditionally made with foot-long snake beans cut into smaller pieces, but sliced runner beans make a great alternative.

 30 minutes    4

- 1 small onion, roughly chopped
- ¼ tsp turmeric powder
- large knob ginger, peeled and roughly chopped
- 4 garlic cloves
- 2 tbsp vegetable oil
- 2 tsp black mustard seeds
- 5 fresh curry leaves
- 1 tbsp mild curry powder
- 400g can coconut milk
- 4 whole cloves
- 1 cinnamon stick
- 1 whole dried red chilli
- 300g/10oz runner beans, stringed and sliced
- juice 1 lime
- 1 tsp garam masala
- handful coriander leaves
- rice and rotis, to serve (optional)

1 In a blender, combine the onion, turmeric, ginger, garlic and 1 tablespoon of the oil together with a large pinch of salt. Heat the remaining oil in a shallow pan. Add the mustard seeds and curry leaves, and cook until they crackle, then add the onion paste and cook until sticky.

2 Stir through the curry powder, then pour in the coconut milk. Add the cloves, cinnamon and the chilli, and bring to a simmer. Tip in the beans and simmer for 15 minutes or until they are tender. Squeeze in the lime juice, add the garam masala, take the pan off the heat and stir through the coriander. Serve with rice and rotis, if you like.

PER SERVING 267 kcals, protein 4g, carbs 9g, fat 25g, sat fat 16g, fibre 4g, sugar 4g, salt 0.2g

Creamy polenta & mushroom ragout

This indulgent main course of Parmesan polenta topped with a rich mushroom mixture and melting Taleggio cheese is ideal for casual entertaining.

 1 hour 5 minutes, plus soaking and infusing   4

- small handful dried porcini mushrooms
- 25g/1oz butter
- 1 shallot, finely sliced
- 2 garlic cloves, crushed
- 5 thyme sprigs, leaves picked
- 500g/1lb 2oz large field mushrooms
- 200g/8oz chestnut mushrooms, sliced
- small glass red wine
- 125ml/4fl oz vegetable stock
- 100g/4oz Taleggio cheese (or vegetarian alternative), sliced

FOR THE POLENTA
- 500ml/18fl oz milk
- 1 bay leaf
- 3 thyme sprigs
- 250g/9oz instant polenta
- 50g/2oz butter
- 75g/2½oz Parmesan (or vegetarian alternative), grated

1 Soak the dried mushrooms in 150ml/¼ pint warm water for 20 minutes. Drain and squeeze, reserving the soaking liquid.

2 Heat the butter in a large frying pan. When sizzling, add the shallot and cook for a few minutes until soft. Add the garlic and thyme leaves, and cook for 1 minute. Turn up the heat and add the soaked mushrooms. After 1 minute, add the other mushrooms and fry over a high heat for 5 minutes. Splash in the wine and boil for 1 minute. Pour in the stock and reserved mushroom liquid, and simmer for 15 minutes until thickened. Turn off the heat.

3 For the polenta, bring the milk to the boil with 500ml/18fl oz water, the bay and thyme. Turn off the heat, leave for 20 minutes, then fish out the herbs and bring back to the boil. Add the polenta in a steady stream, whisking as you go. Cook for 1 minute until thickened, then stir in the butter and Parmesan.

4 Spoon a 'crater' of polenta on to a baking sheet and fill with the ragout. Top with slices of Taleggio and put under a high grill until melted.

PER SERVING 643 kcals, protein 25g, carbs 61g, fat 31g, sat fat 19g, fibre 4g, sugar 10g, salt 1.8g

Veggie moussaka

Lentils take the place of minced lamb in this classic Greek bake, which also makes it low-fat, low-salt and low-calorie – though you'd never guess.

 1 hour 10 minutes   4-6

- 140g/5oz dried green lentils
- 2 onions, halved and sliced
- 2 garlic cloves, chopped
- 2 bay leaves
- 1 tsp dried oregano
- ½ tsp each ground cinnamon and allspice
- 400g can chopped tomatoes
- 1 reduced-salt vegetable stock cube
- 200g/8oz sweet potatoes, thinly sliced
- 1 large aubergine, sliced and the biggest slices halved again
- 250g/9oz low-fat fromage frais
- 1 egg
- 50g/2oz feta, crumbled
- 4 tomatoes, thickly sliced

1 Heat oven to 180C/160C fan/gas 4. Put the lentils, onions, garlic, herbs and spices in a large pan, and pour in 850ml/1½ pints water. Bring to the boil, cover and simmer for 10 minutes.

2 Tip in the tomatoes, stock cube, sweet potato and aubergine, then cover and simmer for a further 20–25 minutes until the lentils and veg are tender and the liquid has been absorbed. Remove the bay leaves.

3 Meanwhile, beat the fromage frais, egg and feta together. Tip the lentil mixture into a large ovenproof dish, cover with the cheese mixture, then arrange the tomatoes on top. Grind over some black pepper and bake for 25 minutes until the topping is set. Will keep for 3 days in the fridge.

PER SERVING (6) 213 kcals, protein 15g, carbs 30g, fat 4g, sat fat 2g, fibre 9g, sugar 13g, salt 1g

Blue cheese vegetable gratin

Simple root vegetables combine with blue cheese to make a satisfying supper.

 40 minutes 4

- 450g/1lb each potatoes, carrots and parsnips, thickly sliced
- bunch spring onions
- large knob butter, plus extra for greasing
- 140g/5oz Stilton
- green beans, to serve

1 Heat oven to 200C/180C fan/gas 6. Cook the potatoes, carrots and parsnips in salted boiling water for 8–10 minutes, until just tender. Drain well.

2 Roughly chop the spring onions. Melt the butter in the pan in which you cooked the vegetables (no need to wash it), add the spring onions and fry gently for a minute or two, until softened slightly. Tip in the vegetables and stir gently until coated with butter. Tip into a buttered shallow ovenproof dish.

3 Slice the cheese and arrange over the top of the vegetables. Bake for 20 minutes, until the cheese has melted. Serve hot straight from the oven, with green beans.

PER SERVING 372 kcals, protein 13g, carbs 43g, fat 17g, sat fat 10g, fibre 10g, sugar none, salt 0.44g

Tomato tarts with roasted garlic & goat's cheese

If you're making these for lunch, get ahead by roasting the garlic the night before and lunch will be ready in no time.

 1 hour 25 minutes   4

- 3 whole garlic bulbs, tops sliced off
- 2 tbsp olive oil
- 375g block all-butter puff pastry, cut into quarters
- 1½ tbsp honey Dijon mustard or use 2 tsp Dijon mustard and a squeeze of honey
- 325g/11½oz cherry tomatoes, halved
- 1 egg, beaten
- 150g pack soft goat's cheese
- handful basil leaves, to garnish

1 Heat oven to 190C/170C fan/gas 5. Sit the garlic bulbs on a sheet of foil. Drizzle over 1 tablespoon of the oil, season and wrap into a parcel. Roast for 50 minutes. Leave to cool.

2 Roll out each pastry quarter and cut into a 14cm/5⅛in-diameter circle. Pop the circles on a baking sheet and score a 1cm border around each edge. Avoiding the border, prick all over with a fork. Chill.

3 Turn up oven to 200C/180C fan/gas 6. When the garlic is cool enough to handle, squeeze the flesh from the bulbs into a bowl. Add the mustard, remaining oil and some seasoning. Mash to a paste with a fork. Spread this over the pastry, leaving the border clear. Top with the tomato halves, skin-side down, and season.

4 Brush the edges of the pastry with the beaten egg, crumble over the goat's cheese and bake for 25–30 minutes until the pastry is golden. Remove from the sheet and allow to cool. Scatter over the basil before serving.

PER TART 591 kcals, protein 18g, carbs 40g, fat 40g, sat fat 19g, fibre 2g, sugar 5g, salt 1.8g

Pea & new-potato curry

. . . .

If you are using fresh peas for this low-fat curry, make a stock out of the pods and use it instead of vegetable stock.

 1 hour 25 minutes   4

- 1 tbsp vegetable oil
- 2 onions, sliced
- 3 red chillies, deseeded and finely sliced
- thumb-sized knob ginger, roughly chopped
- 2 tsp cumin seeds
- 1 tsp Madras curry powder
- ½ tsp turmeric powder
- 750g/1lb 10oz new potatoes, halved
- juice 1 lime
- 500g pot natural yogurt
- small bunch coriander, stalks and leaves separated, each finely chopped
- 200–300ml/7fl oz–½ pint vegetable or pea stock
- 300g/10oz podded fresh peas (or use frozen)
- lime wedges and naan breads, to serve

1 Heat the oil in a large, deep frying pan. Add the onions and cook over a low heat for 10–15 minutes until soft. Throw in the chillies, ginger and spices, and cook for a few minutes. Stir in the potatoes and lime juice, coating the veg in the spice mix.

2 Add the yogurt, coriander stalks and the stock. Simmer slowly for 35–40 minutes until the potatoes are soft and the sauce has reduced. Stir through the peas and cook for another 5 minutes. Sprinkle over the coriander leaves, and serve with lime wedges and warm naan bread.

. . . .
PER SERVING 336 kcals, protein 16g, carbs 50g, fat 8g, sat fat 3g, fibre 9g, sugar 18g, salt 0.5g

Red onion, feta & olive tart

Frozen puff pastry makes a quick case for a tangy, salty filling.

 45 minutes 4

- 25g/1oz butter
- 2 large red onions, finely sliced
- 2 tbsp light muscovado sugar
- 2 tbsp balsamic vinegar
- flour, for dusting
- 450g puff pastry, thawed if frozen
- 100g/4oz feta, crumbled
- 175g/6oz black olives, pitted and chopped
- 1 tbsp extra virgin olive oil
- torn basil leaves, to garnish
- green salad, to serve

1 Heat oven to 200C/180C fan/gas 6. Heat the butter in a pan and add the onions. Add a pinch of salt and fry for about 10 minutes, until caramelised. Add the sugar and balsamic vinegar, and cook for a further 5 minutes, until the juices are reduced and syrupy. Leave to cool.

2 Roll out the pastry on a floured surface and use to line a 30 x 22cm Swiss roll tin. Cover with the onion mixture and scatter over the feta and olives. Season and drizzle over the olive oil.

3 Bake for 15–20 minutes until the pastry is risen and golden and the base is crisp. Scatter over the basil leaves and cut into wedges. Serve with a green salad.

PER SERVING 646 kcals, protein 11g, carbs 53g, fat 44g, sat fat 18g, fibre 2g, sugar 8g, salt 4.07g

Cheesy spring onion tart

Buy a ready-made pastry case to save time. Try asparagus instead of the onions.

 40 minutes   6

- 1 bunch spring onions, trimmed
- 1 tbsp olive oil
- 200g/8oz soft goat's cheese, rind removed
- 150ml/¼ pint double cream
- 3 eggs, separated
- 24cm/9½in ready-made shortcrust pastry case
- tomato salad, to serve

1 Heat oven to 190C/170C fan/gas 5 and heat grill to hot. Put the spring onions on a baking sheet and brush with the oil. Grill for 2 minutes.

2 In a bowl, beat together the goat's cheese, cream and egg yolks until smooth. Whisk the egg whites until stiff and gently fold into the cheese mixture. Spoon into the pastry case and arrange the spring onions on top.

3 Bake for 20–25 minutes until golden. Serve with a tomato salad.

PER SERVING 337 kcals, protein 11g, carbs 18g, fat 25g, sat fat 13g, fibre 1g, sugar 3g, salt 0.64g

Tomato & harissa stew with Cheddar dumplings

Update your veggie casserole with some North African spicing and by adorning it with some cheesy dumplings.

 55 minutes 4

- 1 tbsp sunflower oil
- 1 onion, chopped
- 4 celery sticks, thickly sliced
- 400g can plum tomatoes
- 1 tbsp harissa paste
- 2 large courgettes, halved lengthways and thickly sliced
- 400g can chickpeas, drained
- 1 vegetable stock cube

FOR THE DUMPLINGS

- 25g/1oz butter, diced
- 200g/8oz self-raising flour
- 1 tsp baking powder
- 75g/2½oz extra mature Cheddar, finely grated
- 100ml/3½fl oz milk

1 Heat the oil in a large casserole pan with a lid, then fry the onion and celery for 5 minutes until softening and starting to colour. Tip in the tomatoes and a can of water, then stir in the harissa, courgettes and chickpeas, and crumble in the stock cube. Cover and simmer for 18 minutes until the veg is almost tender. Heat oven to 200C/180C fan/gas 6.

2 Meanwhile, rub the butter for the dumplings into the flour and baking powder with a good pinch of salt, then mix in the cheese with a round-bladed knife. Just 2 minutes before the stew is ready, pour the milk into the dumpling mix and stir with the knife to make a dough. Turn out on to your work surface (no need to flour it), lightly shape into a sausage and cut into eight equal pieces.

3 Put the dumplings on top of the stew and bake in the oven for 15–20 minutes until golden and cooked through.

PER SERVING 444 kcals, protein 16g, carbs 54g, fat 17g, sat fat 8g, fibre 7g, sugar 7g, salt 2.6g

Melanzane parmigiana

This classic Italian aubergine bake is ideal for entertaining and makes a great vegetarian Sunday lunch simply served with a green salad.

 1 hour 55 minutes   4-6

- 2 tbsp olive oil, plus extra for brushing
- 3 garlic cloves, crushed
- 3 thyme sprigs
- 8 large sage leaves, finely chopped
- 4 x 400g cans chopped tomatoes
- 3 tbsp red wine vinegar
- 3 tbsp golden caster or granulated sugar
- 6 large aubergines, sliced lengthways as thinly as you can
- 100g/4oz vegetarian Parmesan, finely grated
- 85g/3oz white breadcrumbs
- 50g/2oz pine nuts
- 2 x 125g balls vegetarian mozzarella, torn into small chunks
- handful basil leaves
- salad and focaccia, to serve

1 Heat oven to 200C/180C fan/gas 6. Heat the oil in a large frying pan, add the garlic, thyme and sage, and cook gently for a few minutes. Tip in the tomatoes, vinegar and sugar, and simmer for 20–25 minutes until thickened a little.

2 Meanwhile, heat a griddle (or frying) pan. Brush the aubergine slices on both sides with olive oil, then griddle (or fry) in batches until each slice is softened and slightly charred. Remove to a plate as you go.

3 In a large baking dish, spread a little of the tomato sauce over the base. Mix 25g/1oz the Parmesan with the breadcrumbs and pine nuts. Top the sauce with a layer or two of aubergine slices, then season. Spoon over a bit more sauce, then scatter over some mozzarella, more of the remaining Parmesan and a few basil leaves. Repeat, layering up – and finish with the last of the tomato sauce. Scatter over the cheesy breadcrumbs.

4 Bake for 30–40 minutes until the top is crisp golden. Rest for 10 minutes, scatter with basil and serve with salad and focaccia.

PER SERVING (6) 481 kcals, protein 24g, carbs 37g, fat 27g, sat fat 11g, fibre 17g, sugar 25g, salt 1.3g

Mushroom, ricotta & rocket tart

· ·

Take all the work out of making a main-course tart by using ready-rolled puff pastry.

 35 minutes   4

- 1 sheet ready-rolled puff pastry
- 2 tbsp olive oil
- 525g family pack mushrooms, halved or quartered if large
- 2 garlic cloves, 1 finely sliced, 1 crushed
- 250g tub ricotta
- good grating nutmeg
- ¼ small pack flat-leaf parsley, leaves only, roughly chopped
- 50g/2oz rocket leaves

1 Heat oven to 220C/200C fan/gas 7 and put a baking sheet inside to warm. Unroll the pastry on to a piece of baking parchment and score a border around the pastry about 1.5cm from the edge. Put the pastry (still on the parchment) on the baking sheet and cook for 10–15 minutes.

2 While the pastry bakes, heat the oil in a large lidded pan and cook the mushrooms for 2–3 minutes, with the lid on, stirring occasionally. Remove the lid and add the sliced garlic, then cook for 1 minute more to get rid of excess liquid.

3 Mix the crushed garlic with the ricotta and nutmeg in a small bowl, then season well. Remove the pastry from the oven and carefully push down the risen centre. Spread over the ricotta mixture, then spoon on the mushrooms and garlic. Bake for 5 minutes, then scatter over the parsley and rocket to serve.

· ·
PER SERVING 461 kcals, protein 13g, carbs 31g, fat 32g, sat fat 14g, fibre 2g, sugar 3g, salt 0.8g

Tuscan salad

. . . .

This rustic, peasant-style salad, traditional to southern Italy, is packed with the flavour of sun-ripened vegetables.

 35 minutes   4

- 2 red peppers, deseeded and quartered
- 2 yellow peppers, deseeded and quartered
- 1 ciabatta loaf
- 6 tbsp extra virgin olive oil
- 3 tbsp red wine vinegar
- 2 garlic cloves, crushed
- 6 ripe plum tomatoes, cut into chunks
- 50g/2oz caper berries or capers
- 50g/2oz marinated black olives
- handful basil leaves, roughly torn
- 2 tbsp pine nuts, toasted

1 Heat grill to hot. Grill the peppers until charred and put in a plastic bag so that the steam loosens the skins.
2 Meanwhile, tear the bread into rough chunks, toast until golden brown and put in a large bowl. Beat together the olive oil, vinegar and garlic to make a dressing; season.
3 Remove the skin from the peppers and cut into chunks. Toss with the toasted bread along with the tomatoes, caper berries or capers, olives, basil, pine nuts and the dressing. Serve immediately on its own or as an accompaniment to a creamy goat's cheese or ripe Brie.

. . . .
PER SERVING 622 kcals, protein 15g, carbs 69g, fat 33g, sat fat 4g, fibre 5g, sugar none, salt 2.68g

Orange & celery salad

Crisp, crunchy textures with fresh-tasting flavours will make this speedy salad a firm favourite.

 15 minutes   4

- 2 large oranges
- 1 small head celery (about 350g/12oz), trimmed, destringed and sliced on the diagonal
- 1 small red onion, cut into very thin wedges
- 200g/8oz red cherry tomatoes, halved
- 85g/3oz lamb's lettuce
- 1 small garlic clove, crushed
- 2 tbsp chopped mint
- 6 tbsp olive oil
- 1 tbsp balsamic vinegar

1 Cut away the peel and pith from the oranges. Cut each side of each membrane to remove the individual segments. Do this over a bowl to catch the juices.
2 Put the orange segments in a large serving bowl and sprinkle over the sliced celery, onion wedges, tomato halves and lamb's lettuce.
3 Add the crushed garlic, chopped mint, olive oil and balsamic vinegar to the orange juice, and whisk until well combined. Season to taste and pour over the salad. Toss well just before serving.

PER SERVING 249 kcals, protein 2g, carbs 9g, fat 23g, sat fat 3g, fibre 3g, sugar none, salt 0.19g

Warm red-cabbage salad

A colourful winter salad with a deliciously nutty dressing.

 25 minutes 4

- 1 tbsp sunflower oil
- 1 red onion, sliced
- 1 small red cabbage (about 350g/12oz), finely shredded
- 1 red apple, cored and cut into chunks
- 1 carrot, grated
- 2 tbsp balsamic vinegar
- ½ tsp light soft brown sugar
- ½ tsp wholegrain mustard
- 4 tbsp walnut oil
- 2 Little Gem lettuces, roughly torn
- 50g/2oz walnut pieces
- flat-leaf parsley, to garnish

1 Heat the oil in a frying pan and fry the onion for 1–2 minutes. Add the cabbage and cook for a further 2–3 minutes. Remove from the heat, and add the apple and carrot.

2 Meanwhile, in a small bowl whisk together the vinegar, sugar, mustard and walnut oil to make a dressing. Season to taste.

3 Arrange the lettuce leaves on individual serving plates. Spoon the warm cabbage salad over. Sprinkle over the walnut pieces and drizzle over the dressing. Sprinkle over the flat-leaf parsley and serve.

PER SERVING 304 kcals, protein 4g, carbs 10g, fat 28g, sat fat 3g, fibre 4g, sugar 1g, salt 0.09g

Noodle & watercress salad

· ·

Use buckwheat soba noodles for extra flavour and colour, although egg noodles would be good, too.

 20 minutes   4

- 200g/8oz dried buckwheat soba noodles
- 2 tbsp light soy sauce
- 2 tbsp sesame oil
- 4 tbsp saké (Japanese rich wine) or dry white wine
- 2 tsp caster sugar
- 8 mint leaves
- 1 large firm mango, halved, stoned and peeled
- 85g/3oz watercress, stalks removed
- 2 tbsp sesame seeds, toasted
- squeeze lime juice

1 Cook the noodles in lightly salted boiling water according to the pack instructions, then drain and plunge immediately into cold water to refresh and stop the cooking process. Put the soy sauce, sesame oil, wine and sugar in a small pan, and heat gently. Remove from the heat and stir in the mint. Set aside and allow to infuse.

2 Meanwhile, cut the mango into fine slivers. Drain the noodles thoroughly and toss with the soy-sauce dressing, mango, watercress and half the sesame seeds.

3 Divide among four serving plates and sprinkle over the remaining sesame seeds. Squeeze over a little lime juice and serve immediately.

· ·
PER SERVING 388 kcals, protein 9g, carbs 53g, fat 16g, sat fat 2g, fibre 2g, sugar 3g, salt 0.04g

Cracked wheat & fennel salad

A delicious combination of roasted fennel and zesty orange, served on a bed of herby wheat.

 45 minutes   4

- 250g/9oz bulghar wheat
- 3 fennel bulbs, cut into wedges
- 4 tbsp olive oil
- pared zest and juice 2 oranges
- 4 tbsp chopped flat-leaf parsley
- 2 tbsp chopped mint leaves
- 4 plum tomatoes, cut into wedges
- 140g/5oz mixed olives, drained
- 100g/4oz rocket leaves

1 Heat oven to 200C/180C fan/gas 6. Put the bulghar wheat in a large bowl, cover with 1 litre/1¾ pints boiling water and allow to stand for 30 minutes. Meanwhile, put the fennel in a large roasting tin, drizzle with the olive oil and season. Add the orange zest and half the orange juice, and roast in the oven for 35 minutes until softened and slightly charred.

2 Drain the bulghar wheat, add the parsley and mint and remaining orange juice. Combine well and season to taste. Put the tomatoes, olives and rocket in a large bowl, add the roasted fennel with the pan juices and toss well.

3 Divide the bulghar wheat among four serving plates, top with the fennel-and-tomato mixture and serve.

PER SERVING 422 kcals, protein 9g, carbs 53g, fat 39g, sat fat 5g, fibre 8g, sugar none, salt 0.03g

Minty broad-bean pâté

So simple to make – serve this fresh-tasting pâté with crusty bread for a snack or light lunch.

 20 minutes, plus resting 4

- 500g/1lb 2oz broad beans, shelled weight, outer skins removed
- 1 garlic clove, very finely chopped
- 150ml/¼ pint extra virgin olive oil, plus extra for drizzling
- pinch ground cumin
- small bunch mint, chopped
- 8 slices crusty wholegrain bread

1 Cook the broad beans in lightly salted boiling water for 10–12 minutes, until tender. Drain well, reserving the cooking water. Transfer the broad beans to a food processor, add the garlic and whizz to a purée, adding a few tablespoonfuls of the cooking water to give a soft consistency.
2 Preheat the grill to hot. Transfer the purée to a bowl and stir in the oil, cumin and mint. Season generously. Set aside for 30 minutes, if possible, to allow the flavours time to develop.
3 Toast each slice of bread on both sides and cut in half. Arrange on individual serving plates. Spoon the pâté on to the hot toast and drizzle over a little extra virgin olive oil.

PER SERVING 413 kcals, protein 7g, carbs 9g, fat 39g, sat fat 5g, fibre 8g, sugar none, salt 0.03g

Bagels with griddled vegetables

If you haven't got a griddle pan, simply stir-fry the vegetables and toast the bagel under a hot grill.

 15 minutes 4

- 5 tbsp olive oil
- 2 red peppers, deseeded and cut into chunks
- 2 courgettes, cut into thin slices on the diagonal
- 4 onion bagels, split
- 2 tbsp balsamic vinegar
- ½ tsp sugar
- 70g bag wild rocket leaves

1 Brush a heated griddle pan with a little of the oil. Add the peppers and courgettes, and cook for 4–5 minutes, turning, until pleasantly charred. Transfer to a plate.

2 Toast the bagels, cut-side down, on the hot griddle pan for 1 minute, until golden. Meanwhile, to make a dressing, whisk the vinegar, sugar and remaining oil together. Season to taste.

3 Put the bagels on individual serving plates and top with the chargrilled vegetables and a handful of rocket. Drizzle the dressing over and serve immediately.

PER SERVING 330 kcals, protein 7g, carbs 32g, fat 20g, sat fat 3g, fibre 3g, sugar 1g, salt 0.72g

Vegetable jalfrezi

Mix up the combination of vegetables in this curry to suit your taste or what's in season – just change the cooking times accordingly.

 1 hour 10 minutes   4

- 1 tbsp sunflower oil
- 2 red onions, thinly sliced
- ½ x 350g jar jalfrezi paste
- ½ butternut squash, peeled, deseeded and cut into chunks
- 1 small head cauliflower, broken into florets
- 1 vegetable stock cube
- bunch coriander, leaves picked and stalks finely chopped
- 500ml/18fl oz passata
- 1 red and 1 yellow pepper, deseeded and sliced
- 400g can chickpeas, drained and rinsed
- 100g/4oz natural yogurt
- 1 green chilli, sliced
- boiled rice and naan bread, to serve

1 Heat the oil in a large frying pan. Add the onions and cook over a low heat for 8–10 minutes until soft, stirring them often and adding a splash of water if they start to stick. Add the paste and mix well, then add the squash, cauliflower, stock cube, coriander stalks, passata and 500ml/18fl oz water. Simmer for 20 minutes, adding some more water, if it gets too thick.

2 Add the peppers and chickpeas, and cook for 15–20 minutes more, until all the veg is tender. Stir in the yogurt and most of the coriander leaves. Serve scattered with the rest of the coriander leaves and the sliced chilli, with rice and naan bread on the side.

PER SERVING 303 kcals, protein 12g, carbs 42g, fat 9g, sat fat 2g, fibre 9g, sugar 23g, salt 1.7g

Walnut & broccoli spaghetti

The walnut mixture will keep in an airtight container for up to 2 days – just reheat it in a dry frying pan.

 20 minutes   4

- 350g/12oz spaghetti
- 200g/8oz broccoli, broken into florets
- 4 tbsp olive oil
- 1 small onion, chopped
- 1 garlic clove, crushed
- 50g/2oz walnut pieces, chopped
- 50g/2oz fresh white breadcrumbs
- ½–1 tsp dried chilli flakes
- 1 tbsp walnut oil

1 Cook the spaghetti in lightly salted boiling water for 5 minutes. Add the broccoli to the pan, return to the boil and cook for a further 5 minutes until both are tender.

2 Meanwhile, heat half the oil in a frying pan, add the onion and garlic, and cook for 2 minutes until softened. Add the walnuts, breadcrumbs, dried chilli flakes and walnut oil, and cook, stirring, until the crumbs are crisp and golden brown.

3 Drain the pasta and broccoli in a colander. Return to the pan, add the remaining olive oil and stir to combine. Divide among individual serving plates. Scatter over the breadcrumb mixture and serve immediately.

PER SERVING 633 kcals, protein 17g, carbs 79g, fat 30g, sat fat 3g, fibre 5g, sugar none, salt 0.31g

Pasta with aubergines

. . . .

Big on flavour but short on effort, this delicious dish is suitable for vegans if you use egg-free pasta.

 25 minutes   4

- 5 tbsp olive oil, plus extra to drizzle
- 2 medium aubergines, diced
- 2 garlic cloves, finely chopped
- 2 tsp cumin seeds
- 1 red chilli, deseeded and finely sliced
- 50g/2oz pine nuts, toasted
- 50g/2oz sultanas
- 350g/12oz tagliatelle
- 6 tbsp chopped coriander
- zest and juice 1 lemon
- grilled lemon halves, to garnish (optional)

1 Heat the oil in a large frying pan. Add the aubergines and cook gently, stirring occasionally, for 10 minutes until golden. Add the garlic, cumin and chilli, and cook for a further 4–5 minutes. Season to taste and add the pine nuts and sultanas.

2 Meanwhile, cook the pasta in lightly salted boiling water according to the pack instructions.

3 Drain the pasta thoroughly and add to the aubergine mixture, along with the coriander and lemon zest and juice. Toss together and serve with an extra drizzle of olive oil and grilled lemon halves, if liked.

. . . .
PER SERVING 627 kcals, protein 15g, carbs 79g, fat 30g, sat fat 4g, fibre 6g, sugar none, salt 0.07g

Tom yam noodles

This simple Thai dish of noodles and vegetables in a tasty broth makes a satisfying supper.

 35 minutes  2

- 1 tbsp sunflower oil
- 1 small onion, chopped
- 2 garlic cloves
- 140g/5oz button mushrooms, sliced
- 1 red pepper, deseeded and sliced
- 2 tsp vegetarian Thai red curry paste
- 700ml/1¼ pints vegetable stock
- 1 tbsp soy sauce
- zest 1 lime and juice ½
- 125g/4½oz egg noodles
- 220g can bamboo shoots, drained
- handful coriander leaves

1 Heat the oil in a pan and fry the onion until golden. Stir in the garlic, mushrooms and red pepper, and fry for 3 minutes. Add the Thai curry paste and cook for 1 minute. Stir in the stock, soy sauce and grated lime zest. Simmer for 3 minutes.
2 Add the noodles to the pan and bring to the boil. Simmer for 4 minutes, until they are cooked. Add the bamboo shoots and most of the coriander, and cook for 2 minutes.
3 Divide the noodles between two soup bowls. Add the lime juice to the broth and season to taste. Pour over the noodles, scatter over the remaining coriander and serve.

PER SERVING 393 kcals, protein 15g, carbs 55g, fat 14g, sat fat 1g, fibre 7g, sugar none, salt 2.77g

Warm crispy-noodle salad

This salad is a riot of colours and contrasting textures, and it's easily adapted to use whatever vegetables you have to hand.

 30 minutes 2

- sunflower oil, for deep-frying
- 50g/2oz crispy rice noodles
- 1 tbsp oil
- 2.5cm/1in knob ginger, chopped
- 2 garlic cloves, crushed
- 100g/4oz sugar snap peas, sliced lengthways
- 1 carrot, cut into matchsticks
- 4 sping onions, sliced
- 175g/6oz spinach leaves, shredded
- 100g/4oz beansprouts
- ½ small cucumber, cut into matchsticks
- 50g/2oz roasted cashew nuts, chopped
- juice 1 lime
- 2 tsp chilli oil

1 Heat 5cm of the sunflower oil in a pan until a cube of bread browns in 30 seconds. Carefully add the noodles, a few at a time, and fry for a few seconds until puffed and crisp. Remove and drain on kitchen paper.

2 Heat the sunflower oil in a wok, add the ginger and garlic, and stir-fry for 30 seconds. Add the sugar snap peas, carrot and spring onions, and stir-fry for 1 minute. Add the spinach and beansprouts, and cook for a further minute, until wilted.

3 Remove from the heat, stir in the cucumber and season. Divide between serving plates and scatter over the nuts and crispy noodles. Squeeze over the lime juice, drizzle over the chilli oil and serve.

PER SERVING 458 kcals, protein 14g, carbs 37g, fat 29g, sat fat 2g, fibre 6g, sugar none, salt 0.6g

Flageolet bean casserole

This recipe is easily multiplied to feed a crowd. The bean mixture can be made in advance and reheated.

 40 minutes   4   Easily multiplied

- 1 tbsp olive oil
- 3 medium courgettes, cut into chunks
- 150ml/¼ pint dry white wine
- 2 x 300g cartons fresh tomato pasta sauce
- 140g/5oz pitted black olives
- 2 x 400g cans flageolet beans, drained and rinsed
- 2 tbsp chopped rosemary leaves
- 50g/2oz vegan spread
- 2 garlic cloves, crushed
- 2 tbsp chopped flat-leaf parsley
- 1 medium baguette, thickly sliced

1 Heat the oil in a large frying pan, add the courgettes and fry over a medium–high heat for 10 minutes, until softened and lightly charred.

2 Add the wine to the courgettes and boil rapidly for 2 minutes, until reduced by half. Add the tomato sauce, olives, beans and rosemary. Bring to the boil and simmer for 5 minutes. Season to taste.

3 Heat grill to high. Combine the vegan spread, garlic and parsley. Spread thickly on to the bread. Arrange the slices on the casserole, grill for 5–10 minutes, until golden, then serve straight from the pan.

PER SERVING 546 kcals, protein 24g, carbs 61g, fat 22g, sat fat 8g, fibre 15g, sugar none, salt 4.35g

Peach Melba pots

This really is a cheat's dessert. Adding a little clove into the mix gives it a mellow warmth, but don't get carried away, as the spice can be quite intense.

 15 minutes 6

- 140g/5oz mascarpone
- 200g/8oz low fat Greek-style yogurt
- 3 tbsp icing sugar, sifted
- pinch ground cloves
- few drops vanilla extract
- 300ml/½ pint double cream
- 300g/10oz raspberry and peach jams – use a mixture
- 3 peaches, each sliced into 8
- 150g punnet raspberries
- 1½ tbsp roasted chopped hazelnuts
- biscotti or amaretti biscuits, to serve

1 Put the mascarpone, yogurt, sugar, ground cloves and vanilla extract in a large bowl. Using a balloon whisk, beat until smooth. Pour in the cream and whisk again until the mixture just holds its shape – you want it to be soft and pillowy, so be careful not to take it too far.

2 Put a little of the jam in the bottom of six small glasses or pots, top with some of the cream mixture, 4 of the peach slices and then more of the jam. Follow this with another layer of the cream, a further drizzle of the jam and finally the raspberries. Can be chilled for up to 5 hours. Scatter over the hazelnuts and serve with biscotti or amaretti biscuits on the side.

PER POT 571 kcals, protein 6g, carbs 39g, fat 44g, sat fat 26g, fibre 2g, sugar 39g, salt 0.1g

Cappuccino mousse

This light, frothy mousse is at its best made with a high-quality dark chocolate.

 15 minutes, plus chilling | 6

- 125g/4½oz dark chocolate
- 1 tbsp instant coffee granules
- 2 tbsp Tia Maria
- 4 medium egg whites
- 140g/5oz caster sugar
- 300ml/½ pint double cream
- cocoa powder, to dust

1 Melt the chocolate in a bowl set over a pan of simmering water, making sure the bowl doesn't touch the water. Remove from the heat and cool. Dissolve the coffee in 2 tablespoons boiling water and stir in the Tia Maria. Stir into the chocolate.

2 In a bowl whisk the egg whites to soft peaks. Gradually whisk in the caster sugar until thick. Stir 2 tablespoonfuls of the meringue into the chocolate mixture to slacken it and then fold in the remainder. Spoon the mousse into six cappuccino cups and chill for at least 20 minutes.

3 Lightly whip the cream and spoon over the mousses. Dust with cocoa to serve.

PER SERVING 461 kcals, protein 5g, carbs 42g, fat 31g, sat fat 19g, fibre 0.5g, sugar 38g, salt 0.22g

Pineapple with rum & raisins

· · · · · · · · · · · · · · · · · · · ·

Some supermarkets sell ready-peeled and sliced fresh pineapple, which will help to speed up this recipe.

 20 minutes   4

- 1 ripe pineapple, peeled
- 25g/1oz butter
- 50g/2oz light muscovado sugar
- 25g/1oz raisins
- 25g/1oz pecan nuts
- 50ml/2fl oz rum
- vanilla ice cream, to serve (optional)

1 Remove the 'eyes' from the pineapple. Cut in half, lengthways, remove the centre core and slice into wedges. Melt the butter in a griddle pan. Add the wedges of pineapple and cook until golden – about 3 minutes on each side.

2 Sprinkle over the sugar, raisins and pecan nuts, and cook until the sugar has melted and becomes syrupy.

3 Carefully pour over the rum and ignite it, using a long match. Allow the flames to die down. Serve the pineapple wedges with the sauce spooned over and a spoonful of vanilla ice cream, if liked.

· ·
PER SERVING 286 kcals, protein 2g, carbs 43g, fat 10g, sat fat 3g, fibre 3g, sugar 13g, salt 0.14g

Mascarpone cream with grapes

Cut the richness of the mascarpone – Italian cream cheese – by combining it with yogurt.

 20 minutes, plus chilling 4

- 150ml/¼ pint red wine
- 50g/2oz caster sugar
- 2 tsp arrowroot
- 350g/12oz seedless red, white or black grapes
- 250g/9oz mascarpone cheese
- 200g/8oz low fat Greek-style yogurt
- 2 tbsp clear honey

1 Put the red wine and sugar in a large pan, bring to the boil and simmer, until the sugar has dissolved. Mix the arrowroot to a smooth paste with a little cold water, then stir into the wine. Boil, stirring continuously, for 1 minute, until thickened.

2 Stir the grapes into the wine mixture, bring to the boil, cover and simmer for 2 minutes. Leave to cool. Spoon into four tall glasses.

3 Put the mascarpone, yogurt and honey into a large bowl, and whisk until smooth. Spoon over the grapes and chill until ready to serve.

PER SERVING 487 kcals, protein none, carbs 35g, fat 34g, sat fat 22g, fibre 1g, sugar 19g, salt 0.58g

Cranberry yogurt ice

A creamy yogurt ice with far fewer calories than regular ice cream. You'll find dried cranberries in larger supermarkets.

 35 minutes, plus cooling 6

- 100g/4oz dried cranberries
- finely grated zest and juice 1 orange
- 500ml/18fl oz low fat Greek yogurt
- 50g/2oz caster sugar
- 150ml/¼ pint double cream
- 3 tbsp brandy

1 Put the cranberries, orange zest and juice and 150ml/¼ pint water in a pan, bring to the boil, then cover and simmer for 25 minutes, until the cranberries are very soft. Allow to cool completely.

2 Beat together the yogurt, sugar and cream until the sugar has partially dissolved. Stir in the brandy and pour the mixture into a freezerproof container. Freeze until thickened – about 3 hours. Stir in the cranberry mixture until well distributed.

3 Freeze until solid. Transfer to the fridge for about 20 minutes before serving. Use within 2 months.

PER SERVING 263 kcals, protein 6g, carbs 12g, fat 20g, sat fat 12g, fibre 1g, sugar 9g, salt 0.18g

Strawberry & rhubarb crumble

A great way to use up strawberries that are slightly past their best – just cut off any blemishes then bake them in this moreish crumble.

 50 minutes   4

- vanilla ice cream, to serve (optional)

FOR THE CRUMBLE

- 140g/5oz plain flour
- 50g/2oz ground almonds
- 100g/4oz golden caster sugar
- 100g/4oz butter, chopped
- 25g/1oz flaked almonds

FOR THE FRUIT LAYER

- 85g/3oz golden caster sugar
- 1 heaped tbsp cornflour
- 450g/1lb strawberries, hulled and halved if large
- 450g/1lb rhubarb, cut into chunky lengths

1 Heat oven to 190C/170C fan/gas 5. To make the crumble, mix the flour, ground almonds and sugar in a bowl, then rub in the butter as though you are making pastry. Tip the mixture on to a large baking sheet and spread out evenly. Create little clumps in the mixture by pinching it together with your fingers, then bake for 10 minutes.

2 Meanwhile, make the fruit layer. Mix the sugar and cornflour together in a large bowl, then toss in the berries and rhubarb until well coated. Tip the mixture into a pan and cook over a gentle heat, stirring until the fruit softens a little and any released juices thicken.

3 Tip the fruit mixture into an ovenproof dish, scraping in all the thickened juices. Add the flaked almonds to the crumble mixture, then scatter over the fruit. Bake for 20 minutes until the fruit is tender and the crumble golden. Leave to cool slightly, then serve warm with vanilla ice cream, if you like.

PER SERVING 667 kcals, protein 9g, carbs 85g, fat 32g, sat fat 14g, fibre 5g, sugar 55g, salt 0.4g

Saffron rice pudding

A simple dessert with the luxurious flavour of saffron.

 35 minutes 4

- large pinch saffron threads
- 175g/6oz pudding rice
- 600ml/1 pint milk
- 300ml/½ pint double cream
- 125g/4½oz caster sugar
- finely shredded zest and juice 2 lemons
- lemon curd and biscuits, to serve (optional)

1 Sprinkle the saffron over 2 tablespoons hot water and leave to soak for 5 minutes.
2 Meanwhile, put the pudding rice, milk, cream, caster sugar and half the lemon zest into a large pan. Bring to the boil, then simmer gently for 20–25 minutes, until the rice is tender and the mixture has thickened. Stir in the saffron-infused water and lemon juice.
3 Spoon into serving bowls and sprinkle with the remaining shredded lemon zest. Serve with a spoonful of lemon curd and biscuits, if liked.

PER SERVING 723 kcals, protein 9g, carbs 81g, fat 42g, sat fat 26g, fibre 0.02g, sugar 33g, salt 0.29g

Passion-fruit teacup puddings

These fruity little puds look lovely served in china teacups, but if you want to prepare them ahead of time and store them in the freezer, make in small sturdy ramekins.

 1 hour 10 minutes   6

- 250g/9oz passion fruit or lemon curd
- 4 ripe passion fruits, seeds and pulp removed
- 3 eggs
- 100g/4oz golden caster sugar
- 85g/3oz butter, melted
- 100ml/3½fl oz milk
- 140g/5oz plain flour
- ½ tsp baking powder
- icing sugar, to dust
- clotted cream, to serve

1 Heat oven to 160C/140C fan/gas 3. Line a large, deep roasting tin with a tea towel and boil the kettle. Put 100g/4oz of the curd in a bowl, mix the remaining curd with the passion-fruit seeds and pulp, and divide among six teacups or ramekins (about 200ml each).

2 Whisk the eggs and sugar together in a large bowl until pale and fluffy – about 5 minutes. Add the reserved curd mix, melted butter, milk, flour and baking powder. Fold together with a spatula until there are no lumps of flour, then divide among the teacups or ramekins.

3 Put the teacups or ramekins in the roasting tin. Fill the tin with hot water from the kettle to halfway up the sides of the teacups/ramekins. Bake for 50 minutes until risen and golden, then cool and chill for up to a day, or wrap in cling film and freeze for up to 2 months. To reheat, bring to room temperature and bake for 15 minutes at 160C/140C fan/gas 3 in a hot-water bath. Dust with icing sugar and serve alongside clotted cream.

PER PUDDING 439 kcals, protein 8g, carbs 52g, fat 22g, sat fat 13g, fibre 2g, sugar 34g, salt 0.5g

Tropical-fruit crunch

Raid the fruit bowl and storecupboard to make this satisfying pud.

 15 minutes 4

- 50g/2oz butter
- 100g/4oz rolled oats
- 6 tbsp demerara sugar
- 4 tbsp desiccated coconut
- 2 bananas, cut into chunks
- 2 ripe mangoes, peeled and cut into chunks
- 225g can pineapple chunks in natural juice, drained
- custard or single cream, to serve

1 Melt two-thirds of the butter in a large frying pan. Sprinkle over the oats, 4 tablespoons of the demerara sugar and the desiccated coconut, and cook for 3–4 minutes, stirring occasionally, until crisp and golden.

2 Meanwhile, melt the remaining butter in another frying pan and add the bananas, mangoes and pineapple chunks. Sprinkle over the remaining demerara sugar and cook over a low heat for 5 minutes, until softened and caramelised.

3 Divide the fruit among four plates and sprinkle over the crunchy oat mixture. Serve with custard or single cream.

PER SERVING 589 kcals, protein 7g, carbs 91g, fat 25g, sat fat 16g, fibre 11g, sugar 16g, salt 0.41g

Almond-nectarine tart

. . . .

This dessert looks spectacular, but using just four ingredients it has got to be one of the easiest to make.

 30 minutes 8

- 140g/5oz white marzipan, cut into chunks
- 5 tbsp double cream
- 375g ready-rolled puff pastry, thawed if frozen
- 4 nectarines, halved, stoned and thinly sliced
- chilled crème fraîche, to serve

1 Heat oven to 200C/180C fan/gas 6. Put the marzipan in a food processor with the cream and whizz to a thick paste. If necessary, roll the pastry out to a rectangle about 30 x 23cm.

2 Lay the pastry on a baking sheet and score a line 2cm inside the edge all around. Spread the marzipan paste over the pastry inside the line and arrange the nectarine slices in rows on top.

3 Bake in the oven for 15–20 minutes, until the pastry is golden and risen. Cut into squares and serve with chilled crème fraîche.

. . . .
PER SERVING 311 kcals, protein 4g, carbs 34g, fat 18g, sat fat 7g, fibre 1g, sugar 9g, salt 0.39g

Honeyed nut & pomegranate pots

This gorgeous dessert uses crushed shredded wheat as a base. When soaked in honey and mixed with pistachios, it tastes just like sticky, sweet baklava!

 20 minutes, plus chilling 8

- 85g/3oz shredded wheat, crushed
- 200g/8oz pistachio nuts, chopped
- 100g/4oz clear honey
- juice ½ orange
- 300ml pot double cream
- ½ x 250g pot low fat Greek yogurt
- 2 tsp rose water
- 110g pot pomegranate seeds

1 In a bowl, mix the crushed shredded wheat with the nuts, 50g/2oz of the honey and the orange juice, then divide among eight small glasses or teacups.

2 Very softly whip the cream, then fold in the yogurt, remaining honey and the rose water. Divide the creamy mix among the glasses or teacups on top of the baklava base. Chill for at least 2 hours, or up to 24 hours. Before serving, top the pots with pomegranate seeds.

PER POT 424 kcals, protein 9g, carbs 25g, fat 33g, sat fat 15g, fibre 4g, sugar 15g, salt 0.1g

Gooseberry & elderflower crumble

The addition of elderflower cordial to the gooseberry filling gives the crumble an extra zing.

 55 minutes 6

- 75g/2½oz butter, diced, at room temperature, plus extra for greasing
- 550g/1lb 4oz gooseberries, topped and tailed
- 175g/6oz caster sugar
- 3 tbsp elderflower cordial
- 175g/6oz plain flour
- 50g/2oz pecan nuts, roughly chopped
- custard, ice cream or cream, to serve

1 Heat oven to 190C/170C fan/gas 5. Grease a 1.2 litre ovenproof dish. Put the gooseberries, two-thirds of the sugar and the elderflower cordial in a pan and cook gently for 5 minutes, until the fruit is soft. Transfer to the greased dish.

2 To make the crumble, rub the butter into the flour until the mixture resembles rough breadcrumbs. Stir in the remaining sugar and pecan nuts. Sprinkle the crumble over the gooseberries and level the surface. Bake for 30–40 minutes, until the topping is golden.

3 Divide the crumble among individual serving bowls and serve immediately with custard, ice cream or pouring cream.

PER SERVING 381 kcals, protein 5g, carbs 57g, fat 17g, sat fat 7g, fibre 4g, sugar 31g, salt 0.25g

Apple & blackberry pudding

A lovely autumn pudding that's easily adapted to use most fruits in season. Serve with pouring cream.

 55 minutes 6

- 75g/2½oz self-raising flour
- 75g/2½oz vegetable suet
- 100g/4oz white breadcrumbs
- finely grated zest and juice 1 large orange
- 5 tbsp milk
- 25g/1oz butter
- 1 large eating apple, peeled, cored and roughly chopped
- 100g/4oz blackberries
- 100g/4oz caster sugar
- pouring cream, to serve

1 Heat oven to 200C/180C fan/gas 6. Sift the flour into a bowl, stir in a pinch of salt, the suet, breadcrumbs, orange zest and just enough milk to make a soft crumble mix.
2 Melt the butter in a large frying pan and cook the apple for 5 minutes, until softened. Stir into the suet mix, then spread into a 1.2 litre baking dish. Sprinkle over the blackberries.
3 Put the orange juice, sugar and 125ml/4fl oz water in a pan. Heat, stirring, until dissolved, then boil rapidly until pale golden. Pour the hot juice over the pudding. Leave to soak for 10 minutes, then bake for 25 minutes. Serve hot or warm with pouring cream.

PER SERVING 286 kcals, protein 5g, carbs 56g, fat 6g, sat fat 3g, fibre 2g, sugar 22g, salt 0.57g

Index

Also available from BBC Books and Good Food

Try 3 issues for just £3

Subscribe to **BBC Good Food magazine** for inspired ideas, reliable recipes and practical tips for all home cooks. Whether you're passionate about cooking, or just love eating good food and trying out a few easy recipes, **BBC Good Food** is the magazine for you.

Every issue includes:

★ Triple tested recipes

★ Inspiring ideas

★ Mouth-watering photography

★ **PLUS** as subscriber you'll receive **exclusive covers** and subscriber only offers

Subscribe today and trial your first 3 issues of BBC Good Food magazine for just £3*